JEROME KERN

JEROME KERN

MICHAEL FREEDLAND

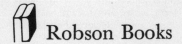 Robson Books

FOR SARA
Who was never lovelier

FIRST PUBLISHED IN GREAT BRITAIN IN 1978
BY ROBSON BOOKS LTD., 28 POLAND STREET,
LONDON W1V 3DB. COPYRIGHT ©1978 MICHAEL
FREEDLAND.

Freedland, Michael
  Jerome Kern.
  1. Kern, Jerome   2. Composers – United States –
  Biography
  784′.092′4   ML410.K/

  ISBN 0–86051–011–5

**Printed in Great Britain by
Biddles Ltd, Guildford, Surrey**

CONTENTS

ACKNOWLEDGEMENTS

No book like this can possibly be the work of one man. The whole process has to begin with the memories of others and sometimes those people go to a very great deal of trouble to provide those reminiscences. To them, my extreme gratitude. At the top of that list must be Betty Kern Miller, who spent so much time with me and went to such a very great deal of bother to provide not just hitherto untold family stories, but also raided the Kern family album for some of the pictures in this book. She was an indispensable guide and help. I am also very grateful indeed to the grand old man of the American theatre, Guy Bolton, and his charming wife, who opened up their home and their memories for me with such wonderful spirit and enthusiasm. Nor can I possibly leave out Fred Astaire (who gave me so much background information and recollections of Kern during my earlier study of his own life and career); Sammy Cahn; Jack Cummings; Louis F. Edelman; John Green (around whose Beverly Hills pool the real groundwork of the two years' research for this book began); Mrs Dorothy Hammerstein; William Hammerstein; the late Johnny Mercer; David Raksin; Mr and Mrs Charles Regensburg; Leo Robin; Richard Rodgers; Arthur Schwartz; and Walter Wager of the American Society of Composers, Authors and Publishers, who opened up the ASCAP archives for me. My thanks, too, to the Librarians of the Lincoln Center, New York; the Academy of Motion Picture Arts and Sciences, Los Angeles; and the

British Library, London; and to Bill Sullivan of the BBC.

For indispensable help in research I must thank Ruth Mindel and my wife Sara to whose patience I owe everything.

Lastly, I cannot possibly omit mention of my secretary-Girl Friday, Alva Robson, who arranged interviews, found hitherto hidden source material, and then saw the whole thing to its final conclusion by typing the manuscript.

London, 1978   MICHAEL FREEDLAND

Long Ago and Far Away

JEROME DAVID KERN survived the immense handicap of not being born on the lower East Side. Indeed, he arrived with at least a silver-plated spoon in his mouth and for the rest of his life, the quality of the silver was only to improve.

Neither of his parents had ever known poverty. They were genteel New Yorkers who had been spared the inconvenience of getting their hands dirty. But they were not members of the Four Hundred either. The list of New York names which formed so important a backdrop to the Social Register of those who were allowed to enter the world of chandeliered society, shunned people like the Kerns. A visitor's card from folk like them left at one of the smart family homes near Central Park would either remain for the rest of the day on the silver salver on which it was left, or would be greeted by a polite message from the butler that his master and mistress were unfortunately out of town.

In that, they were treated no differently from the way that society had reacted to the young Nathan Straus, who founded Macy's department store, Jacob Schiff who reorganized the Union Pacific Railroad, or Felix Frankfurter who was to become a Judge of the Supreme Court. Jews had not yet become accepted as part of the New York establishment.

At the same time, these people themselves paid little attention to the Jews who, like crates of sugar at the wharves on the

3

banks of the East River, were each day unceremoniously unloaded on the reluctant officials of Ellis Island—shawl-clad women with half a dozen wet-nosed children; elderly, bearded men believing that America represented a part-way fulfilment of the prayers for the Promised Land that they offered three times a day in the ghettos of Russia and Poland; and younger men and boys full of the hopes and dreams of youth. Men like Asa Yoelson who was to become Al Jolson, Israel Baline who turned into Irving Berlin, and Morris Gershvine whose son Jacob was to be better known as George Gershwin.

The Kerns were of German stock and, much as the descendants of the Pilgrim Fathers regarded themselves as superior to everyone who followed them onto American soil, the German Jews, in their own eyes, were a cut above these newcomers. Henry Kern had been born in Baden-Baden, but had come to New York as a boy and had made a sizable fortune there. He certainly felt nothing in common with these Jews who so recently had scaled the walls of the ghetto and now lived in windowless tenements and eked out starvation wages from sweat-shops.

The East Europeans were mostly orthodox, people for whom prayer and a supply of ritually-slaughtered kosher food was as important as a bed for the night or a coat for their backs. The longer-established German Jews, on the other hand, for the most part saw that kind of religion as a hindrance on the road to acceptability, a road many of them were now travelling at an increasingly swift pace. It was they who established Reform Judaism, which they considered to be much more consistent with the American way of life of the second half of the nineteenth century.

The 'cathedral synagogue' of that movement was the vast Temple Emanu-El on Fifth Avenue, a place which many of them thought of as a house of high fashion in which to be seen as much as one of worship in which to be heard. The orthodox Jew believed the form of service offered there to be watered down to the extent of losing all meaning. Prayers were recited in English instead of in Hebrew and, worst of all, the men wore no hats. Keeping the congregation in order—that alone would be unthinkable at the noisy, crowded, orthodox establishments which had been transplanted to the East Side from the Old

World like lettuces from one patch of earth to another (and thriving with about the same degree of success)—was Herman Kakeles, born in Bohemia and now beadle to Emanu-El. The orthodox Jews wouldn't have recognized him as such, but to the community of the temple he was a religious man. Yet he did not impose his religiosity on his wife or his daughter Fanny.

Neither of her parents saw any reason why Fanny should not go to as many parties as there were invitations, and they enjoyed seeing her laugh and make a lot of friends. When she met a Henry Kern, a small moustachioed man who looked like her contemporary idol Mark Twain, they could only rejoice in her good fortune. She was plainly in love with him. Their marriage at Temple Emanu-El was the last religious function in either of their lives.

Henry Kern was a business entrepeneur with a gift for adding up figures that immediately turned into large profits. He owned a number of stores, but the retail business was one in which he felt he could make only so much. He branched out and by the 1880s had a highly rewarding contract for cleaning the 5,800 miles of New York City's streets. He hired the equipment, rented the depot and paid people to run the service. He merely looked over the books and banked the cheques. He was, nevertheless, made President of the Street Sprinklers Association.

The Kerns had a happy life in most respects. They entertained an ever-widening social circle and Fanny was usually the chief attraction at all the parties. But life was not all bliss. They wanted a family, and though Fanny had little problem in conceiving soon after their marriage, their first son died shortly after birth. Five more times she became pregnant and five more times her babies—all of them boys—died. But then she was lucky, baby Joseph Kern not only lived but thrived. Less than a year later came Edwin. He too was perfectly normal. Then, late in 1884 Fanny announced that for the ninth time she was pregnant. This latest development was not, however, going to be allowed to spoil Fanny's idea of good living.

The Kerns were keen racing fans—it was, after all, part of the social scene that they enjoyed so much and it would have taken a combination of earthquake and blizzard to keep them away from an important meeting. January 1885 was as cold

5

as only New York winters can be, but not cold enough to deprive Henry and Fanny of a day at Jerome Park in the Upper Bronx, the latest and most splendid thing in fashionable racegoing. Leonard Jerome, the father of Jenny Jerome, whose own claim to fame was as the mother of Winston Churchill, had built it. Jerome was a thoroughbred enthusiast and saw his track as the answer to the recently-opened Belmont Park— except that Jerome Park was intended to be superior, the last word, complete with magnificent silk-draped ballrooms. The Kerns loved it.

On January 27, after a day's racing, the now heavily pregnant Fanny was helped by her husband into the carriage waiting for them outside the track's main entrance, and the couple drove off in the direction of the East River and Sutton Place where they lived in what was then the fashionable part of the New York brewery district. They chatted happily about the races, talked about the friends they had met and about the social calendar that lay before them. Then, quite unexpectedly, came the signs that Fanny knew so well.

By the time that the carriage drew up at Sutton Place and 56th Street, Fanny had to be carried into the house, up the stairs and into the bedroom which had been hurriedly made ready by the parlour maid. Meanwhile, a call went out to the family doctor. Soon afterwards, Fanny gave birth to her child. Once again, it was a boy and once again he seemed very healthy.

Since it had all started at Jerome Park, the couple decided to name the baby after the place. He would be called Jerome— Jerome David. There were few, however, who called him Jerome, even in those early days. When he was very young, he was inevitably 'Baby Jerome' to his parents and 'Master Jerome' to the family's flock of servants. But it did not last long. His two brothers found it easier to call him Jerry, and so did his parents for that matter.

The Kerns were not a musically talented family, although Fanny liked to play the piano. A highly-polished baby grand was as essential a part of the furniture of a prosperous family like theirs as was a set of dining-room chairs. As soon as her sons were old enough to be initiated into the mysteries of musical notation, Fanny arranged for them to have piano lessons. Neither Joseph nor Edwin were particularly adept at playing the instrument, but Jerry looked as though he might be. He showed more interest than they did in listening to the sounds his mother made after she had swept her long skirts away from the pedals, eased her rounded frame onto the piano stool and begun tinkling the keys.

By all accounts, Jerry was happy as a child. He even endured without any particular suffering the velvet Little Lord Fauntleroy suits in which his mother persisted in dressing him—with the accompaniment of long blond curls. It was perhaps Mrs. Kern's way of compensating for having no daughters.

Jerry had a great affection for both his parents, who showered on him all the love and time that wealthy people like them were able to. Not for them the hours at factory benches or business offices away from their children. Both enjoyed being with the boys as much as the children enjoyed their company. That did not, however, mean they were not strict—particularly over the piano lessons.

Mrs. Kern would hover over Jerry as he played, smiling in appreciation of everything he did well and rewarding him with a kiss when he mastered a particularly difficult exercise. But she was ready for the inevitable moment when a finger would stray onto a wrong key or when, through some misplaced sense of musical beauty, he would produce notes that neither the composer nor his piano teacher had intended; then the ruler, she always carried would be rapped down on his knuckles. Years later, Jerry would tell of the notches on the keyboard frame, engraved like initials on a tree trunk, for since Jerry knew what to expect and when to take avoiding action, the piano frequently suffered more than he did.

'Jerry could be a famous musician,' Mrs. Kern told Henry in one of those inspired moments of parental intuition, and from that moment on really considered no other profession for her youngest son. First, though, they decided he must have a completely normal education. They sent him to a private kindergarten, but although they could easily have afforded them, the Kerns decided against private schools for their sons. Jerry and his brothers went to the neighbourhood public schools in New York City.

They had moved now to a three-storey grey house at East

74th Street between Park and Lexington Avenues. Jerry liked
the almost suburban atmosphere of this part of New York, but
most of all he loved the sound of the music coming from the
nearby Episcopalian Church. Since his parents had never
bothered to instill any Jewish religious understanding in him,
they saw no reason to discourage the interest he took in the
services.

The Kerns continued to encourage Jerry with his music
lessons—which he approached with all the enthusiasm of
a soloist about to enthrall the New York critics at Carnegie
Hall. He would sit himself down on the piano stool, stretch out
his hands and play at each lesson with his mother as though he
were Mozart entertaining the King of Prussia. Not even Fanny
Kern believed he was a child prodigy, but she did think he had
more potential than she could deal with herself.

The family changed homes again, this time to Newark, New
Jersey, to coincide with a new upswing in their fortunes. Henry
Kern, still holding on tenaciously to his authority—and the
cash that went with it—with the Street Sprinklers Association,
bought a merchandizing operation called D. Woolf and Co.

The move meant a change of school for Jerry, and also a
change of piano teacher. There was one in the neighbourhood
who had a good local reputation that went with the brass plate
he boasted on his gate. Jerry was enrolled there, and shared
his lessons with a girl of about his own age. A little shy, he
didn't find conversation with girls very easy. However, he did
delight in regaling his young lady colleague with displays of
his favourite trick. As he told her, whenever he was left alone
he liked nothing better than to lie on his back under the keyboard, his arms outstretched and hands playing the piano keys
above him—while his shoulders manipulated the pedals.
Whether or not this had anything to do with a later affliction
in his neck has, as far as anyone knows, not been established.
As it was, it was doubtful whether his teacher knew about his
favourite pastime.

As Jerry got older, he had to change schools again—this time
to Newark High School. Soon, it became clear he was the best
student to play the piano and the organ for daily assembly. He
was also asked to try his hand at writing music of his own. It is
little known that the first compositions ever to bear the name

Jerome David Kern were for the shows of Newark High School. Alas, no trace remains of them. (For that matter, apart from one, there are no manuscripts of any other Kern work, either. No one pretended these earliest Jerome Kern compositions were the greatest music of the kind ever written, but in the vernacular of the time, one teacher told him: 'Jerome, you are an all-round whizz.'

He was no great student in any other subject, although he showed a lively curiosity in things that interested him—such as ancient pottery, or an early book. But because of his musical abilities, he was shown an indulgence which in those late-nineteenth-century times was unusual. His teacher also appreciated the fact that while waiting to graduate, he was taking evening classes at the New York College of Music, studying theory and orchestration.

'I'm going to be a composer,' he told his parents, and Mrs. Kern knew that her prophesy was going to be fulfilled. Her husband was not so sure. After all, he reasoned, who could make money writing music? He was content to indulge the boy's whims while he was studying. Privately, however, he had other plans for young Jerry, and when the boy was 16, after continuing his studies at the New York College, Mr. Kern broke the devastating news: 'I'm taking you into the business,' he declared. Jerry protested, but Henry Kern's word was law.

His first job was to attend an auction. Jerry was so bored with the whole proceedings that he drifted into a deep sleep. The trouble was that while dozing off, his head nodded so vigorously that D. Woolf and Co. became the proud owners of so many boxes of prunes that they had to be taken away in a couple of horse-drawn carts. It wasn't deliberate—Jerry was not that sort of boy—but he might have been forgiven for thinking that perhaps this was a good way of persuading his father not to extend the family business. Henry wasn't convinced—but he did allow Jerry to continue his evening classes, learning piano with Alexander Lambert and Paolo Gallico, and harmony under Dr. Austin Pierce and Albert von Doenhoff. One day, Jerry told himself, he just knew he would be as famous as they were.

His father remained unimpressed. If his son could buy prunes that no one wanted, how much more successful would

9

Jerry be when purchasing something for the business that he himself wanted badly? Henry Kern smiled to himself at what he considered to be another example of his smart business acumen. He had heard that an Italian company had just brought over a consignment of pianos from their own country. 'Get me a couple of them if you think they're worth it,' ordered Kern Senior, 'and let's see how they sell.'

For once, Jerry was being presented with an opportunity that seemed to be more fitted to his personal interests. He felt even happier when he was ushered into the imposing sale room by people who were the essence of Italian hospitality and kindness. He saw the pianos standing before him. The woodwork was polished like no other pianos yet seen in America. Their keyboards were a blinding black and white.

'Yes,' he said, 'I'll take . . .'

'No,' said the owner, who knew precisely what he was doing, 'first we eat and drink a little.'

Jerry was taken into the dining-room above the store where a bottle of chianti was opened and the wine poured generously into his glass. The scuingilli and calamari and other Italian delicacies were irresistible. Finally, the piano importer suggested they talk business. Jerry was plainly in no fit state to talk about anything, other than the warmth of the hospitality, and the glow he felt from the food and wine. 'Yes,' he said, 'I'll take two . . .'

'Two hundred?' said the man. 'Bravo!'

The following morning, pianos started arriving in profusion at the Newark premises of D. Woolf and Co.

'Son,' declared the elder Kern when the news broke that his furniture venture appeared to be on the verge of ruin, 'I think I'm going into the piano business. As for you, I think you should become a musician.'

Who?

HENRY KERN knew when he was licked. If Jerry was more interested in making music than in making money, he and Fanny could afford to indulge him. Neither Joseph nor Edwin was showing much progress in the family business either and there was little point in having the merchandizing house filled with people who hated every moment they spent there.

But the big question to settle was: with what kind of music was Jerry going to concern himself? Fanny was persuaded that her Jerome was going to become the American Tchaikovsky. Jerry himself was not so clear. Certainly, he loved the melodic strains of the great composers, but he liked, too, the popular ballads that daily came off the ships from Germany and England and were as eagerly awaited as if they were some life-saving drugs—which, in a way, they were.

The American theatre could not have lived without a constant transfusion of new material from Europe. These were the songs sung and whistled on the street corners of New York and in the corridors of establishments like D. Woolf and Co. Songs like 'Goodbye Dolly Gray', the hit tune of the Boer War, 'Tell Me Pretty Maiden' from the show *Floradora*, and 'The Tale of the Kangaroo', known in Germany as 'The Burgomeister'.

His parents were a little concerned about his affinity for the theatre. 'Never,' his father warned him solemnly, 'marry a show girl, Jerry. They are not nice.' He promised that he would not. At the moment, he was more interested in the theatre's music than in its girls. Whether consciously or not, Jerome Kern was making up his mind that this was the kind of music that interested him. His grades at the music college were not proving him to be a new Tchaikovsky. His piano playing was highly competent, but there was nothing to indicate he was a genius. His composition showed some interesting traces, but did not persuade anyone that he was going to be a writer in the great classical mould. All he knew for sure was that he wanted to be involved in music, to surround himself with musical people and listen to music all day long.

At home, he sat at the piano and scribbled away the hours, producing a note here, refining it there. Like other hopeful teenagers of every era, he sent off bundles of papers to a succession of music publishers. All were returned—until, when he was 17, in 1902, the Lyceum Music Publishing Company wrote him a letter without sending back all his manuscript papers. They told him they were going to publish a piano piece he had written called 'At The Casino'. For the first time, printed sheet music bore the legend: 'By Jerome D. Kern'.

Henry Kern was impressed. If Jerry were going to write music, he must study so that he could write the best possible music. At their home one night, Henry told his son: 'Jerry, you're going to Europe'—which even a man whose sole connection with the art was the sudden arrival on his hands of 200 unwanted pianos, knew to be the centre of the music world.

Jerry went to Berlin—which he hated, finding it cold, stiff and full of people who considered themselves the intellectual superiors of anyone from that quaint upstart place called America. However, there were advantages; the theatres of the Friedrichstrasse were playing first-hand the shows that were drawing more than half the crowds on Broadway, and he bought tickets to sit and take in everything around him. Heidelberg was more to his taste, and the Bavarian countryside enchanted him. He also found the musical theory and the composition lessons there to be of such a high standard that he could decide only to practise one day what they were preaching.

In London's Strand he went to performance after performance at Daly's and the Gaiety Theatre. It was the beginning

12

of a love affair with London, which claimed to be the hub of the universe and he really thought it was. It was lively, gay and to his way of thinking, extremely civilized. New York paled in comparison, it was provincial and oh, so dull.

Back in New York in 1903, he decided that the time had come to unleash himself upon a theatre world which he assumed would be avid to hear his music, music that was so influenced by all that he had picked up on his travels. After all, it was unusual enough for American composers to be so well-travelled.

The 18-year-old was shown the door in every office he entered. However Charles K. Frohman, one of the greatest impresarios of his age, did actually speak to Jerry: 'I do not buy American music,' he told him. 'I get all mine from England.' Jerry decided to turn to the Lyceum Music Publishing Company, the firm which had seen 'At The Casino' bury itself without trace. They liked his spirit. It took guts for one of their own writers to knock on the door and say he had come to inquire about the job 'that my associate told me about'. There was no associate, but there was a job. Jerry was hired at $7 a week as a song plugger. When he told his mother about it, she was less than happy. Now even she recognized that he was unlikely to become a Tchaikovsky.

It was a tough life, plugging songs. Long before the coming of radio or the mass distribution of records, the publishers' offices were the places where the new songs were given their first public try-outs. Theatrical impresarios came to listen to tunes that they might be able to use in their coming shows. Vaudeville artists called to pick up a number that they would sing in the coming season—and, who knows? perhaps find themselves a signature tune for life. They heard the songs played in any one of a dozen or more booths that were rarely particularly soundproof, by young men who enjoyed their work so much that they never expected to be well paid into the bargain—a situation happily exploited by the publishers. The best pluggers were those who played the loudest—so that a dancer heard only the notes coming from the worn upright piano in the room in which he was improvising his steps, or a singer could read over the lyrics printed on the sheet music in his hand and so picture immediately the way he would be interpreting them, without the distraction of any tinkling keys from next door or two or three booths down the corridor.

Kern began to impress the people who came to hear him. 'I'll have the little kid with glasses and the curly hair,' some of them would say. And the little kid with glasses and curly hair was always ready to oblige. Soon, however, Jerry was moving on. The Wanamaker department store wanted a pianist to plug the Lyceum's music. Each day, they would give over time for leading publishers to exhibit their wares—and Jerry was chosen for the Lyceum's afternoon spot.

Every afternoon, he would arrive to take the place of Jean Schwartz, who was to become famous as composer of Al Jolson songs like 'Rockabye Your Baby With A Dixie Melody' and 'Chinatown My Chinatown', and go home just before his piano stool was taken by Ernest R. Ball, who was to write 'Mother Machree', 'When Irish Eyes Are Smiling' and 'Let The Rest Of The World Go By'. Since Schwartz invariably left early and Ball was nearly always late, Jerry had the piano and the Wanamaker crowds to himself most of the time.

You couldn't keep a spirit like Jerome Kern's under the wraps of other people's ideas for long. When there was a phrase or a part of an arrangement he didn't like, he'd take out his pencil, make the changes that he was convinced would improve the piece, and play them the way he wanted them to sound. The store didn't object to this; how could it, when it was plain that customers who were out looking for a bedroom suite, for example, stopped in their tracks in the music depart-ment and just stood and listened. They stayed to buy music, and were in a better mood then to start thinking about that more expensive piece of furniture they had earlier spurned. Also, the fame of the 'entertainment' that the store provided had spread, and was attracting custom.

Nowhere, however, was the reputation of this music 'service' greater than in the entertainment business. Marie Dressler, then approaching the peak of her fame as a musical comedy entertainer and not yet contemplating the success she would before long have in Hollywood, heard about it and asked Wanamakers to lend her a pianist to accompany her own performances. 'I need a pinch-hit accompanist right away,' she said. The young Kern was happy to volunteer; and she

14

was delighted with the way in which he could turn frequently indifferent material into the sort of stuff that had the audiences eating out of her large, expressive hands. She asked him to write her a few songs; the tunes cut no real ice, but her audience seemed to like them. Webber and Fields, the famous comedy pair, asked him to supply them, too, and he was thrilled to do so.

But he wanted to move on. At East 22nd Street, he climbed the brown stone steps leading up to the offices of T. B. Harms and Co. and was shown into the room of the president, Max Dreyfus. In his frock coat and striped black trousers, he was the most splendid figure that the young Kern had seen since he had entered the world of music. Jerry was used to seeing musicians with dirty, frayed cuffs, long, untidy hair and fingernails that showed a scant acquaintance with soap. But the spectacle that greeted him now made him decide that this was an establishment of class, and he wanted to be part of it.

'I'm Max Dreyfus,' said the elegant figure.

'I'm Jerome Kern,' said the young visitor, 'and I want to imbibe the atmosphere of music.'

It took about six months for Kern to discover the reason for the immaculate appearance of the president that day. Mr. Dreyfus used to get five dollars for playing the piano at parties and he was about to go to work.

Jerry in the meantime became a 'general utility' man at the Harms company for about $12 a week—making out invoices and signing letters. Before long, his terms of employment were extended, and he was sent out selling music to stores in the Hudson Valley. Dreyfus was impressed with the results of this venture. He said afterwards: 'He was so full of youthful spirit and had withal a certain charm that the minute he showed up, doors opened wide for him.'

But the young Kern above all wanted to sell his own music inside those doors. He had saved much of the money he had earned with the two publishers. Now he was going to spend it on another trip to London. There, he was sure, he would make his fortune, though that, like most things, was not quite so easily settled. He did, however, have the sense to go to one of the American companies established in London—because they too, believed that everything of importance happened in the West End before it happened on Broadway.

Charles Frohman, as we have seen, was one of these. Fortunately for Jerry, Frohman was not in London when he called at the office, brandishing his one published song and full of the experience that had made him—as he claimed—so successful on Broadway. 'You can have a job,' the London office manager told him. 'We will pay you to produce some songs we can put into our London shows. You'll get £2 a week.' London was cheaper than New York and in 1903, £2 was more than $10. He took the job.

It was a time when no self-respecting theatregoer dreamt of arriving before the curtain had been up for at least half an hour. Therefore the dullest songs and the corniest jokes were assembled for this part of the show—when they were usually performed for the benefit only of the poorer people in the gallery or in the pit at the back of the stalls. And that was Jerry's job: to write songs that no one of importance would ever hear—let alone remember. The first of these was sung by a pretty 17-year-old American girl called Billie Burke at the Pavilion Music Hall (a few years later she was to achieve international stardom in a show called *The School Girl*, and then marry Florenz Ziegfeld).

It was, however, essentially a period for sharpening his musical wits and developing his theatrical connections. Seymour Hicks, one of London's biggest musical comedy producers, bought a bundle of the inconsequential numbers that Jerry wrote at the time. He also introduced him to a comedian-singer called George Grossmith, one of the greatest entertainers of the British stage and a favourite of Gilbert and Sullivan. When he heard the young Kern play, Grossmith said: 'You play divinely, with a tremendous gift of tune.' He could, he told his friends, fill the shoes of Lionel Monckton, Paul Rubens and Leslie Stuart, all big names of the British theatre.

Kern was gratified, but he wanted to get back to America. He sailed first-class to New York, at about the time that a Seymour Hicks show, *Mr. Wix of Wickham*, was making the same journey. It was due to open at the Bijou Theatre on Broadway on September 19, 1904. The story—about an English emigrant to Australia who convinces people that he is heir to a fortune—was considered adequate, but the score by Herbert Darnley and George Everard was anything but.

16

Hicks suggested Kern might be interested in 'Americanizing' the project. When the show opened, Jerry made an impact for the first time. The critic Alan Dale wrote: 'Who is this man Jerome Kern, whose music towers in an Eiffel way above the average hurdy-gurdy accompaniment of our present-day musical comedy?'

Jerry decided to look for more ways of getting his work across to the theatre managements which, despite the plaudits for *Mr. Wix*, were still reluctant to give whole musical scores to an unknown teenager. He went back to work for Mr. Dreyfus, now as his personal assistant, and at the same time got a job as a rehearsal pianist in a number of Broadway theatres.

Rehearsals on Broadway could be horrendous experiences. The same tunes would be played over and over again—until not only the stars but even the composers and lyricists couldn't bear to hear them again. It was then that Jerry usually turned idly to an entirely different tune.

'What's that?' the producer inevitably asked. And Kern would answer: 'Oh, just a little something I did myself.' By that time, anything sounded better than the original number, and Jerome Kern had sold another song.

The 'little something' in another transplanted Seymour Hicks show, *The Earl and the Girl*, starring Eddie Foy, was called 'How'd You Like To Spoon With Me?' It had lyrics by Edward Laska. Laska and Kern had had a fleeting acquaintance at the New York College. They met again at the Harms office one day when Laska—at 20, a year older than Jerry—was impatiently waiting for two men with whom he was writing a show, Sam Lehman and George McManus (who was much later to become famous all over America for his comic strip 'Bringing Up Father').

As he waited in the publisher's ante-room, Kern recognized his former fellow student. 'What are you doing here?' he asked, and Laska told him about the successful career he considered he was already carving out for himself as a lyricist. He had had a number published and featured in a show called *The Girl and the Bandit*. His song was 'Sweet Little Caraboo', and was sung in a Red Indian scene. The producer, Frank L. Perley, liked it so much that he had given him the title of the next song he wanted him to write. 'Call it,' he had said, ' "How'd You Like

To Spoon With Me?" ' Spoon was the 'in' word at the time and was the nearest that polite society of the early years of the century would get to what later became known as 'necking', 'petting' or simply 'making love'. It was also a lot easier to rhyme with 'moon' and 'June'. Perley's idea was that the phrase could be burlesqued beautifully by a man and a woman so huge that outside the grand opera stage they could never be taken seriously.

Jerry looked almost a musical comedy character himself that day. The young man who had so much admired the impeccable elegance of Mr. Dreyfus was in his shirt sleeves, and perched on his head was a straw hat with no top that looked rather like a can of fruit after the lid had been shorn off. There was an unlit cigar in his mouth on which he puffed incessantly, kidding neither Laska nor himself that it was alight or that he was really adult enough to smoke it. As he puffed, he pounded the piano and scribbled a few rough notes of music. Years later, Laska was to say: 'All I had to do was throw this rather absurd phrase at Jerry Kern and he had a complete melody in the making.'

If Laska is to be believed, Kern not only had the melody worked out but the verse, too, and they had agreed on a partnership—if only for this one tune. With that, his new partner took a pad, scribbled a dummy lyric, and went home to develop his theme. As the years went by, the lyricists would change but, with one exception, the working pattern would not.

Getting the number into Perley's show took too long for the impatient Kern. After sitting with Laska outside the producer's office for the best part of a morning, he tapped the lyricist on the shoulder and said: 'Let's find another producer.' Of course, it was totally unethical, but an ambitious 19-year-old could not afford such scruples. They took it to Alf Hayman of the Frohman organization, but he turned it down. 'They won't know what "spoon" means in England,' he explained. Kern and Laska crossed the road to the office of the Shubert Brothers, who were presenting the Broadway version of *The Earl and the Girl*. They said they'd buy the song and use it in their show. It turned out to be not only a tuneful melody and verse with a witty lyric, but the way it was presented, the song was one of the most spectacular numbers yet heard coming

18

from any stage. As the chorus sang, three girls in the briefest of flimsy skirts, the frilliest of petticoats and the sheerest of black silk stockings sat on flower-entwined swings and swung themselves out into the auditorium.

The *Dramatic Mirror* said of the 'Spoon' song: 'It is the most successful number ever introduced here.' It became the talking point among the theatregoers of New York. One man reported: 'I remember hearing Jerry Kern whistling that song when we were at school in Newark together.' Whether he had or not, it made an interesting topic for debate.

It was 1905, and Kern couldn't wait to get back to England. In London, he worked on another Hicks show, composed some more music, and met Charles Frohman again. 'You know, young man, you English compose better music than the Americans do,' Frohman told him. 'Would you consider coming to America with me?'

'I might do that, sir,' said Jerry, touching his forelock, and he went on writing more songs that would be lost without trace. But it was good training for a young man who intended to make his career in the theatre. He learned that the sort of music he wanted to write could not be fitted into a play without his first knowing something about the show itself. Even at this early stage, he was beginning to have an influence on the theatre. Kern was the first to see that a show's tunes should not be totally separate from everything else. In England, musical comedies had been all sound and no spectacle—costumes, scenery, the general appearance of the show being secondary to the music and the laughs. In America, it was always the other way round. It didn't matter what it sounded like so long as it looked good. Lyricist Otto Harbach, who has described Kern as 'one of the great dramatists', said that in those early days, songwriters 'paid almost no attention to plot. They were indifferent to characters, even to the situations in which their songs were involved. They didn't care much about the kind of lyric that was being written for their melodies, just as long as the words could fit the tune.' At the age of 20, Jerry was trying to change all that. He was also getting to know more important people.

He was working as a rehearsal pianist at Daly's Theatre and at the Aldwych, and continuing his efforts to get his work into shows. At Daly's, three Kern songs were interpolated into a production called *Catch of the Season*—'Molly O'Halleran', 'Won't You Kiss Me Once Before I Go' and 'Raining'.

It was at the Aldwych Theatre that, sitting in his shirt-sleeves and playing poker with some of the cast rehearsing a show to be called *The Beauty of Bath*, Kern was introduced to a man who was to play an important part in his life: P. G. Wodehouse. Pelham Grenville Wodehouse, born of an upper-class English family, had gravitated from writing short stories for magazines to writing for the theatre, and although he would return to his short stories—Jeeves then was little more than a soda-syphon's spray away—he loved both the atmosphere of the stage and the songs.

He wanted to meet Kern, whose name rarely appeared on a theatre programme but who had a reputation, as he put it, which inspired people 'to seek him out when a job must be done'. He knew Jerry was beginning to be known in the trade as 'Dr. Tinkle-Tinker', a man who could improve tunes and make them sound less like something that Franz Lehar had left behind. Wodehouse had ambitions as a satirist, and the British politician, Joseph Chamberlain, seemed to be fair game. 'Why don't we work together?' he suggested to Kern. 'We'll write a song called "Mister Chamberlain" '. Kern saw no reason not to agree. After all, everyone was talking about Chamberlain's protected-tariff policy, and Wodehouse had given him a title. Now he hummed a few bars, went to the piano, and before very long was ready to hand the music to his new lyricist. That done, the song went to his ever-appreciative friend Seymour Hicks. 'My good fellow,' said Hicks, 'I'll honour you by singing it in *The Beauty of Bath*.' The song had ten encores on the first night.

Jerry went along to the show and cheered with everyone else. It was much better than the Gilbert and Sullivan operas that were still the rage of sophisticated London, but which Kern hated. 'They are so monotonous, saccharine and tinkling,' he decided.

While Frohman provided him with his American work, the impresario George Edwards was very much Kern's English godfather. For him, Jerry wrote most of the score of *Venus 1906*, which is generally accepted to be London's first revue.

Jerry not only enjoyed the English theatre, he admired the style of the English to the point of Anglicizing his own behaviour and dress. He wore a stiff white collar, smartly creased trousers —pressed in the front, that is, not at the sides as the older generation wore them—and affected a Homburg hat similar to the one worn by the King. He always carried a cane.

One day, walking down the Strand, he came across a gang of workmen busy on a building site. 'Who is the foreman here?' he demanded authoritatively, pointing his cane at one of the men.

'I am, sir,' said a beefy man, raising his cloth cap respectfully.

'Well, my man,' said Jerry. 'We have decided not to proceed with this work any further today. You may all go home.'

'Thank you, sir,' said the foreman, marching backwards and continuing to touch his cap as he did so. 'Thank you, sir.' He told his fellow workers, and the gang 'clocked off' at two o'clock in the afternoon.

Certainly, it was not easy to take young Mr. Kern for anything but an Englishman—unless you listened very carefully, that is. Charles Frohman, for one, had no idea that he was anything other than British. Once more, he pressed his offer: 'Why don't you come to work for me in America?' and this time, Kern said 'Yes'.

Little Eva

THEY CROSSED THE ATLANTIC together, the seasoned producer, Charles K. Frohman, and the bright-eyed young 'English' songwriter whom he liked to think of as his protégé, playing cards in the first-class saloon. Frohman liked Kern's lively sense of humour, and shared his contempt for the tunes the ship's orchestra were painfully presenting for the benefit of the well-heeled passengers.

On the fifth day, as the ship steamed up the Hudson, Frohman called Kern to join him on deck to admire the New York skyline coming into view. As they sailed through the Bay, Frohman nudged the apparently suitably-impressed Kern. 'That, my boy,' he said, 'is the Chrysler Building. Over there, the "Flat Iron Building". I bet you didn't know that Manhattan is really an island? And that you have to take a carriage across the bridge to get to Brooklyn!' Jerry was diplomatically agog. 'Well, bless my soul,' he replied in his very best English voice, 'how marvellous actually to see America.'

As they walked down the gangplank at the pier, a broad New York voice called out: 'Why, Jerry Kern. Haven't seen you since Newark. Is your father still selling pianos?' Frohman was incredulous. By the time Kern took out his United States passport to show to the immigration control man, his incredulity had turned to outrage. Fortunately he did not allow it to spoil his relationship with a man he knew would bring in customers to his theatres. 'Better meet me at my office in the morning,' he said. 'I suppose you can find your way there on your own!'

In the 1906 production, *The Little Cherub*, Jerry had 'Meet Me at Twilight', 'A Plain Rustic Ride' and 'Under The Linden Tree'. And then later that year there was a show called *The Rich Mr. Hoggenheimer* for which he wrote 'Bagpipe Serenade', 'Don't Tempt Me', 'Don't You Want A Paper Dearie', 'I've A Little Favor' and 'Poker Love'. As the months passed and the number of shows increased, so did the demand for Kern songs. Early in 1907 there was *The Dairymaids*, for which Jerry wrote a whole album of songs ranging from 'Little Eva' (a tune that he would have special cause to remember) to 'I'd Like To Meet Your Father'.

For Jerry, life was highly satisfactory. He was doing what he enjoyed, and being paid for it. But then came his first real taste of personal sadness. His mother was struck by cancer, and died on December 31, 1907. There were no New Year's Eve celebrations for him that year, or any other year. The Jewish faith, of which he never consciously felt himself a member, marks the anniversaries of parents' deaths as days to be remembered and ones on which celebrations should be avoided. Probably without realizing there was any religious custom involved, he kept meticulously to this tradition, and went into quiet seclusion every New Year's Eve.

There was to be another, similar, date in his diary. Exactly eight months after Fanny's death, on August 31, 1908, Henry Kern died of pernicious anaemia. Jerry was overcome with grief. Although he had two elder brothers, he made himself responsible for the supervision of their graves in the cemetery at Salem Fields.

He steeped himself in his work—new Frohman shows in which he was interpolating songs in the same way as a worker on Henry Ford's assembly line would soon be adding a nut and bolt to a car. And like the car, the show might have gone on the road without all the added bits and pieces he could provide, but with far less chance of success.

However, he was finding time for other diversions—and not simply in the card-rooms set aside in every decent music publishing house or producer's office. Jerry had found himself a girl, a dark-haired actress named Edie Kelly, who had the curvacious 'hour-glass' figure fashionable in the Edwardian period. Jerry knew that in pursuing Edie, he was near to breaking the promise about show girls that he had made to his father, but she was irresistible. He doted on her, took her with him to the theatre, to restaurants, to the races and to ball games. He spent about $30,000 on Edie in a year—almost everything left him by his father. Then at the end of 1909, Edie informed him it was all off. She was marrying someone else.

Jerry was distraught, but managed to lose himself in his work. There were more shows for Frohman, shows with titles like *The Girl and the Wizard*, *Kitty Gray*, and George Grossmith's *The Dollar Princess*. For the latter show, he produced 'Not Here, Not Here' and 'A Boat Sails On Wednesday'. Perhaps it was this song that persuaded him to return yet again to England.

He breathed in the smoky air of London and felt immediately at home. Most of all, of course, he loved the London theatres where dukes still went to drink champagne out of the slippers of chorus girls and where the music sounded just that little bit old-fashioned. Working in England, Jerry Kern wrote in the style of the English composers—but only to a point. Even then, there was that little extra something that made his work different—different enough to please Frohman, who knew what would appeal later to the audiences on Broadway.

In the summer, when he was not thinking about the theatre, he spent his days by the river. In his elegant straw hat and striped blazer, it was as difficult for casual acquaintances to believe that Jerome Kern was the American Frohman had found him to be. At Walton-on-Thames—then a sleepy village with a population of 13,000, but a couple of generations later virtually to become a London suburb—Jerry and his close friend Laurie Grossmith called in at the Swan Hotel. In 1909 it was a typical English inn, more pub than hotel, and famous for the Cheddar cheese and pickles that went with the best draught beer in Surrey.

The Swan was especially popular because George Draper Leale, the landlord, was the perfect host. He also prided himself on being a good father; that was evident to anyone who saw the strict way he supervised his 18-year-old daughter Eva and her two sisters. Leale did not, however, object to their following the current craze for bicycling, providing they were adequately chaperoned, and it was seeing Eva cycling down a leafy lane not far from the Swan that first made Jerry forget his erstwhile love, Edie. Later he found an opportunity to talk to her at the Swan. She was not pretty in any conventional sense. Certainly she didn't have Edie's figure, nor did she have Edie's witty conversation, but she was attractive and responded politely when Jerry spoke to her. Leale knew a little about Kern's background and did not disapprove of their talking together—providing, that is, he was always in a position to eavesdrop on their conversation.

Eva may not have been the epitome of sophisticated womanhood, but she had another quality which appealed to Jerry. There was a certain innocence about her that he had never found in the society women to whom he had been introduced at the Café Royal, or in the girls of the theatre. But she was not afraid to talk.

'And what work do you do, Mr. Kern?' she asked as Jerry looked admiringly into her dark eyes.

'I am a composer,' he said, expecting her to be immensely impressed.

'And what do you compose?' she asked.

'Well,' he said, 'I have recently written a song called "Little Eva".' Miss Leale looked at him suspiciously, but Kern did not notice. 'And you may have heard of a song I wrote before that called "How'd You Like To Spoon With Me?"'

The title sounded to Eva like an indecent proposition. She reacted accordingly. Looking him straight in the eyes, she said: 'I cannot abide a liar!' and walked away.

Kern had to persuade her that he had neither been lying nor making an indecent proposal. Not only would that have precluded any development of their relationship, but it would have ruined his reputation in those parts—and Jerome Kern was very concerned about his reputation. He wooed Miss Leale as though she were a combination of Gaiety Girl and Princess, plied her with flowers and compliments, and sent her a copy of some sheet music with his name encircled in the corner. Eventually, she smiled sufficiently to make him know that even if she did not quite believe him, she did not altogether consider him a bounder and a cheat. Finally, he sent her a

25

telegram saying he was going back to America. She kept it in a box. It was the first wire she had ever received. Eva—or rather Mr. Leale—had agreed that he could write to her.

Back in New York, Jerry wrote his first note to Eva. When it arrived, she dutifully presented it to her father to read first. When he was satisfied that it contained nothing indecent or indelicate, he allowed his daughter to read it. Jerry sent her more letters, and photographs, one daringly enough signed with his 'love'. Eva wrote back to Jerry and, like the letters she received, she had to show each one to Mr. Leale before it was posted. Occasionally, however, she was not above posting letters without Papa's approval. In one of these, she told Jerry about her father's role as censor—and suggested that perhaps he might like to consider writing two letters in the same envelope, one that Mr. Leale could read and one that he would not. She waited anxiously for the arrival of the postman, took from him the letter bearing the American stamp and tore open the envelope in her father's presence. As she handed Mr. Leale the letter that was for his eyes, she surreptitiously hid the more personal note in her capacious sleeve. It was her very first love letter. In it, Jerry told her he was returning to England.

When he arrived, he caught a train straight to Walton. But it was Edward Leale he saw first—to ask for his daughter's hand in marriage. How could Mr. Leale resist such correct behaviour? On October 25, 1910, Kern and Eva were married in a simple ceremony at St. Mary's Church, Walton-on-Thames. Jerry saw no reason not to go through the Church of England rites and the vicar had no objections to a Jewish bridegroom being married according to the usages of Christianity.

Eva looked forward to and thoroughly enjoyed the transatlantic voyage. For a girl whose idea of an evening's entertainment had been a gathering around the parlour piano at the Swan Hotel, the glamour of the ocean liner was beyond the bounds of her imagination. Jerry taught her deck games and in the first-class restaurant of the ship indicated which wine she should drink with the dish of the evening. Later, in the ballroom, they danced and listened to the music which Jerry was even more convinced was distinctly inferior to anything he could write himself.

However, much as she had enjoyed the voyage, her first

glimpse of New York was horribly intimidating. She was bewildered from the moment that they cleared customs and Jerry's horse-drawn carriage was summoned. Everything looked so big and, as they rode from Downtown to Up, so dirty. Jerry had told her that they had a small but comfortable home to go to, but for the first few nights, they booked into an hotel— her husband had allowed three out-of-work actor friends to stay at his bachelor apartment on West 68th Street and now they were reluctant to move out. When the couple did finally get vacant possession of the apartment, there were even more traumatic experiences awaiting the young, unsophisticated Mrs. Kern. According to the often-told family story, as the door was opened by Jerry's maid, Mary, Eva found difficulty in stifling a scream. Mary was black—the first black woman she had seen in her life.

The effect of her new environment was to make Eva grow steadily more inhibited. She was frightened of doing the wrong thing, and in such strange surroundings, it was difficult to know exactly when she was infringing convention. She didn't like leaving the apartment, but even less did she enjoy staying there while Jerry was away. Mary was a constant source of problems. She exploited the fact that the new mistress of the house was ill at ease, and in effect, when Jerry was not about, Mary made it clear it was she who was the boss. She had been in Mr. Kern's employ for years before this upstart girl from England arrived on the scene, and she was taking no orders from her now. Every time the haughty Mary swept from one room to the next with a duster or a brush, Eva cowered. As the days went by, she grew more and more annoyed by Mary's behaviour, yet there seemed little she could do about it. However, when the maid sat at the piano and started pounding out a simple keyboard exercise, Eva was furious enough to speak out.

'Mistah Jerry said I could,' replied Mary, and that was the end of Eva's protest. When Jerry got back that night, he thought it very funny indeed. Eva sometimes felt, in fact, that he was not taking her problems seriously enough. He loved going out to parties every evening, while Eva felt too new to this strange country to want to do anything but stay at home, tinker with the piano herself and hope that Jerry would get into the habit of staying home and playing for her.

27

Gradually, however, Eva cured herself of her fears. As she stepped out into the still warm New York air and began tentatively to explore the sidewalks, a lot of the excitement she had felt at the outset of her journey across the Atlantic returned. This was a wonderful place, she decided. She was in love with America again. She was also very much in love with Jerry, who was as busy as ever writing songs for Frohman shows—his most recent had been *The King of Cadonia* which featured titles like 'Every Girl I Meet', 'Hippopotamus' and 'Coo-Coo'. But most memorable of the productions of the period was *Our Miss Gibbs*, for which Kern wrote 'Eight Little Girls', 'Come Tiny Goldfish To Me' and 'I Don't Want You To Be A Sister To Me'.

Those 1910 shows were followed the year after by *Little Miss Fix It* which starred the famous Broadway duo of Nora Bayes and Jack Norworth and included the Kern 'Turkey Trot' to words by Norworth. Another success was 'There Is A Happy Land'. The shows all came from abroad, and Jerry was still being used principally as a 'Mister Fix It'. He was also supplementing his income with a series of articles for the *Musical Courier*. He didn't sign any of them, and more of an attraction than the miniscule fees he received was the fact that he could get free tickets for concerts.

But bigger things were about to happen. The Shubert Brothers had been keeping an eye on him ever since he had first excited Broadway audiences with 'How'd You Like To Spoon With Me?' Now they made him an important proposition: would he write the *bulk* of the score of a new show with which they were going to open a new theatre? It was not the sort of challenge Kern could lightly turn down. Though he was not expected to write every piece of music for the show, this time he would be the main composer. A man who had made his name from interpolations in other people's productions could not now object when there was additional material inserted into his. Now other composers would write the incidental pieces at the beginning. *La Belle Paree*, like every other Broadway show before it, would be heavily influenced by the European style but Kern's directive was to make it American, too.

The Winter Garden, built on the site of the former horse exchange and near where the streetcars turned round, was going to be the most magnificent theatre that America had ever known. It was all plush velvet and silk drapes, and rumour had it that there was a spot in the centre of the stage where a whisper could be heard at the back of the balcony. In fact, the early reviewers of the show concentrated more on the theatre itself than on the performances they saw. 'The walls and balcony front are in old ivory and gold and the ceiling marked off in latticed squares in old ivory behind which is an artificial sky of blue,' noted *The New York Times*. *The Times* also was thrilled with the receptacles for cigar ash at the back of each seat. As for the music, well, the paper was kind enough to point out that Miss Jean Alwyn was 'one of the cleverest of artists' and that Miss Alwyn's first song (it was called, in true European fashion, 'The Edinboro Wiggle') was killed by a particularly long drawn-out and tedious scene between three comedians. No mention was made of the composer of the piece —or of any of the other songs in the show—not even of a number called 'Paris Is A Paradise For Coons' sung by a young lady named Stella Mayhew and a blackface artist making his Broadway debut who called himself Al Jolson.

Jolson's part in *La Belle Paree* came so late that he walked home from the theatre after the show finished at midnight, feeling that his short-lived career was in tatters. Only a few kind words from *The New York Times* next morning persuaded him he had been anything but a failure. The Shuberts put Jolson on earlier in *La Belle Paree* the next day and the rest, as they say, is history. A year later, Al was calling himself the World's Greatest Entertainer, and no one argued.

Recognition for Jerome Kern came more slowly. As far as most Broadway cognoscenti were concerned, it was an adequate contribution to a so-so production at a splendid new theatre. He was lucky to have Al Jolson to sing a couple of his songs, and the Shuberts obviously felt their young composer had come up with what they wanted. To his delight they asked him if he would like to do more. Meanwhile, he went back to helping to fix other people's material.

From the piano at the apartment in West 68th Street came numbers like 'Hoopla-La' and 'I'll Be Waiting At The Window' for the show *The Girl from Montmartre*, and 'Mind The Paint' and 'If You Would Only Love Me' for Arthur Wing Pinero's

Mind the Paint Girl. The fact that Kern wrote the title song gives an indication of his rising status. But for most of the time, Jerry's name was missing from the programmes. 'As long as my name is on the cheque, I'm happy,' he said, though there was a nagging feeling at the back of his mind that he ought by now to be thinking about making a reputation for himself as a composer in his own right rather than simply as a mender of other people's mistakes.

Eva was quite determined about this. Now that she had come to terms with America, she wanted to be known as the wife of America's most famous composer. It was one of the few arguments Jerry allowed her to win. At her insistence his name was featured on *all* the programmes as well as on the published score for the production—and on the cheques.

But then came what most people in the theatre regarded as the supreme accolade—a request from Florenz Ziegfeld to write a number for the *Ziegfeld Follies*. Only a couple of years before Jerry received his 'summons', the Follies had established themselves as the most luxurious, the most extravagant productions seen on any stage—the best acts in vaudeville, the finest sets, the most mangificent costumes, the most beautiful girls—girls whose bust, hip and waist measurements were never allowed to deviate from the specifications that Ziegfeld himself had decreed. Ziegfeld was as fussy about the music he required as he was about the visual impact of his productions. When Jerome Kern was asked to write for him, it was a meeting of two minds. His song—note the spelling—'I'm A Crazy Daffudil' was the hit number of the evening every time it was played.

By that time, about 30 Broadway shows had had the benefit of 100 Kern songs, including Ziegfeld's next production *A Winsome Widow*, produced in 1912. For this, Jerry was accorded the privilege of writing just one number—appropriately, 'Call Me Flo'. No greater compliment could have come from Flo Ziegfeld, who in reality would allow no one to call him anything but *Mr*. Ziegfeld.

As always, the lyricist—and there could be four or five different men writing the lyrics even if only Kern and the show's main composer were working on the music—handed Jerry an idea for a title which sparked off a notion for his music.

The words would be filled in later on. Jerry was well paid for his work now that he was no longer tied to the Frohman stable. If, later on, he was to describe himself as a 'musical clothier', making songs to conform to his client's needs much as a tailor shapes a suit to measure, Jerome Kern had learned already that a song had first to have something that suited the particular show on which he was working.

When the producer asked for music, Jerry delivered—but first he wanted to know all about the plot. *The Red Petticoat* in November 1912 was, more than any previous show, a vastly important event for Kern. For the first time, he provided the entire score for a play—a show that wowed them at Daly's Theatre and sent *The New York Times* into ecstasies. And, this time, it did not omit to mention Jerry's name. The show was billed as a melodrama, but, said *The Times*, '*The Red Petticoat* is better as musical comedy than melodrama.' It must have owed something to Sweeny Todd, the 'Demon Barber of Fleet Street', although in this case the barber was a girl wearing the said red petticoat assisted by six other young ladies in garments of different hues. ' "The Boys Of Grandmama",' reported the paper, 'sung with its flute and clarinet obligato, is possibly the daintiest of all the tunes which Jerome Kern has written for the piece, and the Misses Dupree, Laboulaya, Le Meer, Barry, Lee and Barneto help to gladden the eye. But there are other tunes to please, soothing and melodious and occasionally of a sort well calculated to heighten the effect of a comedy lyric.'

Jerry never seemed to have to wait for inspiration to come, and if he did take time with a song, then it was spent in tidying up the notes to give the rounded sounds he wanted. Eva was delighted to see him so content—although she did tend to think he was spending too much of his time at those parties which she hated so much and from which she would try to escape whenever possible. She also began to wonder why she had not yet become pregnant. It was rare in those early years of the century for a couple not to produce children within a year of marriage unless something was very wrong indeed.

As far as Jerry was concerned, he could not wait to get on to the next show and the next score—songs for *The Doll Girl*

('When Three Is Company') and for *Miss Caprice* ('Look In Her Eyes'). Then later in 1913 came *Oh, I Say*. Actually, there was not a lot you could say about *Oh, I Say* except that for the first time, Jerome Kern used his knowledge of orchestration to take the American musical out of the very comfortable rut into which it had sunk. He decided that it needed more than a pleasant pit orchestra fiddling away to make people sit up and start whistling the tunes on their way out of a theatre. So for numbers like 'I Know And She Knows' and 'Katy Did', he did what no one else had done in a theatre before. He introduced the saxophone—in fact, two of them. Not only did the saxophone soon become an accepted part of every theatre orchestra, it became part of the fabric of American life. It has since come to be accepted as the epitome of the jazz age, the sound of the Roaring Twenties. Kern used it seven years before that decade arrived.

Just as he liked to feel that the orchestra playing his music was fully under his control, so he began seriously to think of the role of that music in a complete show. 'Every song,' he said, 'has to tell a story.' So naturally enough, for his tune 'The Old Clarinet', the saxophone took second place to the reed instrument in the song.

Jerome Kern was by now the talk of the business. When, in 1913, a group of songwriters decided that the time had come to protect their interests, he was among the first to be contacted. The trouble was that all over America, music from shows was being played in restaurants and in ballrooms, in clubs and in parks, and the poor composer got not a nickel for his contribution to the entertainment of the masses. A copyright act had become law in 1909 but no one paid any attention to it and it was virtually unenforceable. It was Puccini, in America for the world première of *The Girl of the Golden West*, who started the ball rolling towards a better deal for the songwriter. 'How much,' he asked, 'will I earn from the performances of my music in restaurants and nightclubs?' When his publisher, George Maxwell, told him, 'I am afraid, nothing,' the Italian was furious. Maxwell decided that something had to be done, and he contacted Victor Herbert, then regarded as the doyen of American composers. Herbert was annoyed, too, and made it his personal responsibility to get the situation changed.

He called 35 of those whom he considered to be his leading competitors and collaborators (composers, lyricists and publishers, including Jerome Kern) and in October 1914 invited them to dinner in a private room at Luchow's restaurant on 14th Street. He had not, however, bargained with New York's Fall climate. The night of the dinner, the pavements of the city were awash, and it was impossible to move on the streets without running the risk of being blown by the wind into the path of oncoming street cars. Nevertheless, nine intrepid guests did turn up. Jerry was not among them. The nine decided to give their absent colleagues a second chance. They called another meeting for February 13, 1914 at the Hotel Claridge. Kern again accepted the invitation—and this time he was among those who attended.

After a magnificent meal the assembled diners agreed to join the organization founded four months before by Victor Herbert and his eight colleagues—the American Society of Composers, Authors (i.e., the lyricists) and Publishers. From that moment on, the Society was known simply as ASCAP. By attending the dinner, Jerry became a charter member. Few people would in the years to come benefit as much as he did by his decision. ASCAP issued licences to theatres, hotels, restaurants—all the places likely to play the music of its members. For a set fee, the licensee was given permission to perform the copyright material of any member of ASCAP— who was then paid royalties according to the number of times his work was played. In later years, every radio and TV station in the country would pay for an ASCAP licence.

It was an important year, and not just for the music industry. America tried to convince itself that it was more bothered by the introduction of income tax than about the war breaking out in Europe. The American newspapers were full of the activities of an evangelist called Billy Sunday—the man who, in the song, tried to shut down Chicago—and the dance halls were echoing to the sound of the tango.

As far as the theatre-going public was concerned, the attraction that pulled the crowds in August, 1914—a ridiculously hot time of the year in which to launch a new theatrical production—into the Knickerbocker Theatre was *The Girl from Utah*, starring one of the most beautiful girls on the

Broadway stage, Julia Sanderson. The show was produced by Charles Frohman and the music was listed as being by Paul Rubens and Sydney Jones—'with additional numbers by Jerome Kern'. *The Girl* had already succeeded well enough in London, but, as usual, Frohman wanted an American touch for what was after all an American story—about a young woman's attempt to avoid becoming just another wife of a Morman polygamist. As they opened their programmes that night, few gave much thought to the title of one of those 'additional numbers'. It was called 'They Didn't Believe Me'.

And no one who wasn't actually there to hear it for himself would have believed the impact that the song made that night. By the time Julia Sanderson was into her final chorus, the audience was singing along with her:

> *'And when I told them how wonderful you are*
> *They didn't believe me. They didn't believe me . . .'*

The lyric came from Herbert Reynolds, who had thought it so good that he wanted to sell it to Al Jolson, then swiftly approaching the peak of his success in the theatre. But Kern knew that Jolson would belt it out from the footlights up to the top of the gallery, dance with it, whistle it and get down on one knee with it, and he thought it needed to be put over more simply, as a ballad. So he included it in the Frohman production—together with 'I'd Like To Wander With Alice In Wonderland' and 'Why Don't They Dance The Polka Anymore?'

It was, of course, 'They Didn't Believe Me' that gave *The Girl from Utah* an important spot in the history of the American theatre, even if the show did only play for 120 performances—which was just 'fair to middling' in Frohman's judgement. When Jerry's ASCAP colleague, Victor Herbert heard it, he was generous in a way that few songwriters ever are about their rivals—although he allowed himself what he doubtless considered to be a certain justified immodesty. 'That man,' he said, 'will one day inherit my own mantle.' It would be charitable to suppose that he had no inkling of the understatement that really was.

Sitting Pretty

IN SHOW BUSINESS as in any other walk of life, it is very often more a question of who you know rather than what you know. In mid-1914, Jerome Kern had good reason to be glad that he knew Elizabeth Marbury. Miss Marbury—known to everyone as Bessie—was the only female agent and theatrical producer in New York. She not only wanted Jerry to work for her, she also had a lyricist whom she was sure would be an ideal partner. His name was Guy Reginald Bolton.

Bolton was 30 years old, born in Broxbourne, Hertfordshire, in the English Home Counties, and Bessie was astute enough to realize that that would immediately earn him the favour of her young composer, who was just a year older. She may not have bothered to add that Bolton had American parents—in fact, his father, Reginald Pelham Bolton, was an eminent engineer. Guy himself had studied to be an architect, but he had a much greater facility for dashing off story lines and lyrics for imaginary songs than for detailed technical drawings.

Why not, suggested Bessie, link up and write her a show? She already had a star for the production, a popular Broadway beauty called Marie Cahill. It was an offer that both thought wise to accept. Bessie acted as their agent, and Daniel V. Arthur produced. Their show, *Ninety in the Shade*, opened at the Knickerbocker Theatre on January 15, 1915. It was not a notable success. The songs—'Where's The Girl For Me?',

'I've Been About A Bit' and 'Wonderful Days', among others—were hardly brilliant and the whole production ran for no more than 40 performances. But it did prove one thing—that the two men got on well and could form a working partnership.

Ninety in the Shade had not been the original show that they discussed. In the first place, Bolton had been asked to revamp a 1905 London production called *Mr. Popple of Ippleton*; with *Ninety in the Shade* out of the way, they could get round to doing it. By the time the two of them had thrashed the idea around in their minds, they had not only changed the title to *Nobody Home* but had come up with a completely changed story line and book as well as a brand new basket of songs. Nobody now remembers 'Why Take A Sandwich To A Banquet?'—and it is probably fortunate for Jerome Kern's place in the history of the modern American musical theatre that they don't—but 'You Know And I Know' remains a veritable delight.

Kern and Bolton, however, had not been the first choice for the job. Bessie Marbury had wanted the finest musical talent to provide the greatest songs and there was only one man, she believed, who could really fit that bill—Victor Herbert. Herbert, however, was unattainable—the sort of money he demanded needed a packed auditorium at the New Amsterdam Theatre every night to justify paying it, and that was not her idea at all. Bessie Marbury wanted an intimate type of show that required an intimate type of theatre—and she had just the right place ready and waiting to be filled: the Princess.

The Princess was on 39th Street—a tiny little playhouse with only 292 seats. But even so, it was not the easiest establishment to fill. Certainly, you couldn't produce a *Ziegfeld Follies* Show there, but theatregoers liked to feel they were getting quality whatever it was they were seeing, and so far the Princess had not been able to come up with the right formula. Kern and Bolton, Bessie felt, were the answer to what both she and her partner in the Princess enterprise, Ray Comstock, had in mind.

Once *Nobody Home* had opened, there was no doubt that the collaboration had worked beyond their wildest hopes. Guy Bolton remembers: 'Jerry was very good for someone like myself to work with. He had a great instinct for the theatre.

I'd write a play and then discuss it with him. He was essentially a showman. George Gershwin [with whom Bolton was later to work in shows like *Lady Be Good* and *Oh, Kay!*] was not.' 'What kind of backdrop are you having for that scene?' Kern would ask Comstock, even though he had only one small number planned for what was technically known as a 'stage wait'—while the scenery was being changed. He wanted to be sure just how his song would fit into the whole production. Between them, Kern, Bolton, Paul Rubens (who shared the book and lyrics with Bolton), Comstock and Marbury had made a very significant change in the American theatre. Together, they had introduced small musical comedy that was not small-time and begun a genre that in various forms would continue during the next decade and be known in the business simply as the 'Princess Shows'.

There was something particularly elegant about the shows. 'When we agreed to do them, we decided to write the word "charm" up above our desks,' Bolton explained. 'And those shows really were charming.' Charming and, in their way, expensive—although no costly stars were imported and the size of the orchestra matched the dimensions of the stage. But Bessie Marbury spared nothing on the sets and the costumes. One of her close friends was Elsie De Wolfe, wife of the British baronet, Sir Charles Mendel. She was a brilliant set designer and had worked on an even earlier Bolton show called *Polly with a Past*. To match the elegance of Miss De Wolfe's sets, Bessie imported the finest costumes from Paris—all made-to-measure for her performers with not a seam out of place, and nothing but the sheerest silk used for the dresses. She believed that people would go to the Princess to see the sets and the costumes just as much as they went to watch the performers or listen to the music. It was a belief that Jerry Kern shared.

Nobody Home demonstrated his conviction that songs had to be integrated with the plots. It may seem strange now, but until then a comedy in which the jokes came solely out of the action was virtually unknown. Just as in a British pantomime, characters would tell funny stories that were as divorced from the plot as were most of the songs. In *Nobody Home* both songs and jokes were fitted into the story of an Englishman falling in love with an American show girl.

In addition to 'You Know And I Know', there was one other number that made a big impression—even though it was not to last as a 'standard'. It was called 'The Magic Melody'. It certainly made an impact on Carl Engel, a man whose musical knowledge—he gloried in the title musicologist—impressed the most hidebound of theorists. Writing of the song and its composer, he said: 'A young man gifted with musical talent and unusual courage has dared to introduce into his tune a modulation which has nothing extraordinary in itself, but which marked a change, a new regime in American popular music. It was just the thing that the popular composer in the making had been warned against by the wise ones as a thing too high-brow for the public to accept. They were the foolish prophets. The public not only liked but they went mad over it. And well they might for it was a relief, a liberation.'

With the success of *Nobody Home* ringing as loudly in his ears as the tunes in the memories of the Princess's patrons shuffling their way through the exits, Jerry was asked by Comstock and Marbury for more of the same. But he no more wanted to be tied down to a successful formula than he would have wanted to repeat a flop.

Charles Frohman suggested that he might like to go with him again to England, to see a few shows and play a round or two of golf. He knew Jerry had learned the game on his last trip to London—when he equipped himself with a superb set of hand-made clubs, the plus-four trousers that were *de rigueur*, and a book called *How To Play Golf*. He took up the game as thoroughly as he had learned his trade—and had a hole-in-one on his first day on the course to prove it. Jerry, of course, never needed to be asked twice to go to London. It would also be an opportunity for Eva to see her parents again.

The Kerns and Frohman decided to sail for Liverpool on May 1, 1915, on the pride of the Cunard Line, the S.S. Lusitania, described by the shipping line as 'the fastest and largest steamer now in Atlantic service'. But under the advertisement making those claims in *The New York Times* was another headed 'Notice'. It warned that 'Travellers intending to embark on the Atlantic voyage are reminded that a state of war exists between Germany and her allies and Great Britain and her allies; that the zone of war includes the waters adjacent to the British Isles; that in accordance with formal notice given by the Imperial German Government vessels flying the flag of Great Britain or any of her allies, are liable to destruction in those waters and that travellers sailing in the war zone on ships of Great Britain or her allies do so at their own risk.' The advertisement was signed by the Imperial German Embassy, Washington D.C., April 22, 1915.

Few people took much notice of that warning, believing that it applied only to military traffic, and the Lusitania was a passenger liner with no military cargo—although years later there would be evidence that the ship did carry munitions. Certainly neither Kern nor Frohman thought they had any reason to worry about it.

On the night of April 30, Jerry, with a crowd of theatre friends around him, played the evening away—a good game of cards after a splendid dinner, followed by the composer delighting his friends with his latest offerings. The echo of laughter mingling with his own pleasant piano playing was the sweetest sound that Jerome Kern knew. Certainly, he didn't want to waste those precious moments by going to sleep. As far as he was concerned, the night began at 2 to 3 a.m. and lasted until noon.

On May 1, he got up at 11 o'clock. Eva knew she must never wake her husband, and the servants had similar instructions. The trouble was that the ship was due to sail at 10. Jerry was angry with himself for over-sleeping. Eva was instructed to make another booking—but at a sensible time when the tide suited their own living habits. Frohman meanwhile was making himself comfortable on board ship. He had been one of the first to go on board. Soon after his arrival, a telegram had been received by the ship's wireless operator. A similar one had come for another distinguished passenger, Alfred Vanderbilt. The captain saw the messages and decided not to pass them on. Both warned that the men should disembark immediately. Whether they had come from people who were really in the know, were simply reactions to *The New York Times* advertisement, or were from others who just had a hunch, will never be known for sure. The passengers did not receive the telegrams, and the ship left the pier at noon.

Six days later, off the coast of Ireland, the Lusitania was

39

torpedoed. Charles Frohman and Alfred Vanderbilt drowned. Had it not been for Jerome Kern's notorious love of late nights, he would doubtless have gone down with them—and would scarcely be remembered as more than a songwriter who, like thousands of others, had had his work performed on the stages of London and New York, although he had created a much loved standard called 'They Didn't Believe Me'.

As it was, he and Bolton decided to work on another show for the Princess, although first he had two other commitments to fulfill—*Cousin Lucy*, staged at the Cohan Theatre, with book by Charles Klein and lyrics by Schuyler Green, for which he wrote 'Those Come Hither Eyes' and 'Two Hearts Are Better Than One', and *Miss Information* which opened at the same theatre just over a month later. That featured the famous Elsie Janis and Melville Ellis, but even their presence couldn't breathe enough life into the show for it to last for more than 47 performances.

Its songs were pedestrian—'Banks Of Wye', 'A Little Love But Not For Me', 'Some Sort Of Somebody' and 'The Mix Up Rag'. What was important was that the show represented Kern's professional introduction to Charles Dillingham—a gentleman among the uncouth moguls who controlled the Broadway theatre. While the other impresarios tied their employees and artists to contracts that all but strangled them, Dillingham showed a paternal interest in those he retained and employed. True, he made money out of them, but none ever felt he had been cheated.

On the other hand, Bessie Marbury and Ray Comstock might well have begun to feel that they were being cheated of the services of Kern and Bolton—had there not been the satisfaction of knowing there was another Princess collaboration on the way. And one that finally left no doubt that what Kern and Bolton were creating was making a lasting impression on the American theatre. It was called *Very Good Eddie*.

Now it seems a perfect caricature of the musical of the 1920s, the sort of production to be guyed so perfectly 30 years later in *The Boy Friend*—two young couples, both on their wedding day, getting separated on the steamer taking them off to their honeymoon hotel. One bride—tiny—is left on shore with the other girl's husband, also tiny. The second bride—

large—commiserates with the first girl's stranded husband, who is also large. After a series of predictable misunderstandings on the way, the couples end up in the same hotel but in wrong bedrooms; since, of course, the marriages have never been consummated, there is not the slightest problem getting an annulment and the right couplings made in the sight of God and the law.

With the exception of one number, 'Babes In The Wood', the tunes were not spectacular Kern. And the lyrics were far from the best that Guy Bolton had produced; but every one of them merged into the plot as though they had been fitted together like a piece of some intricate jigsaw puzzle.

Very Good Eddie was a title which rolled easily off the tongue; Fred Stone used it constantly in his ventriloquist act, Montgomery and Stone, and it became the catchphrase of every gay young thing convinced that he (or she) was bright and very much up-to-the-minute.

There was deliberately no star part in the show. Had there been one, it would have thrown the entire budget out of control. Instead, Ernest Truex, Jack Hazzard, John Willard, Ada Lewis and Alice Dovey shared the honours between them. What was more, there were no more than two sets. Nor did the Princess stage have enough room for a conventional large chorus. In its place, there were ensemble quartets and sextets and the orchestra itself was of a kind never seen before in a show that filled a theatre to capacity every evening. Frank Sadler, who was working for Kern as his orchestrator, arranged the music so that it needed no more than 11 musicians. Instead of making it seem like a cheapskate production, all these factors were carefully blended together to provide a degree of sophistication that was totally new. People who paid their money at the Princess box office usually left at the end of an evening feeling as though they had been privileged to attend a private soirée.

Bessie Marbury and Ray Comstock knew they were onto a huge financial bonanza. The whole production cost no more than $7,500 to stage, and that sort of money was recouped within a couple of weeks.

Years later, Guy Bolton would see something very similar to his plot—it was written in conjunction with Philip Bartholomae, on whose story *Over Night*, it was based—in Noël Coward's *Private Lives*. The two writers met on board ship soon after the *Private Lives* triumph, and Bolton told Coward how similar he thought the two plots were.

'Do you think,' asked Coward, puffing at a cigarette through a long holder, 'that the authors of *Very Good Eddie* could have seen *Private Lives*?'

'No,' said Bolton, 'I don't think so, because *Very Good Eddie* was written in 1915 and *Private Lives* in 1930!' Bolton says he has no reason to believe that Coward had seen *Very Good Eddie*, either.

A lot of people, however, did see it. The show was a tremendous success. Years later, Richard Rodgers was to say that as a boy of 14 he went to see *Very Good Eddie* and became convinced that his future lay in writing show music of his own. The effect, he said, was 'shattering'. But on the first night the attention of both Kern and Bolton as they restlessly walked up and down the promenade section at the back of the auditorium, was focused on the audience, straining to see a smile here, a frown there on the faces of the customers, and all but measuring the length of applause for each number. One member of the audience in particular, an Englishman, made an impression on Bolton. In the book based on their years of collaboration together, called *Bring On The Girls*, the Englishman (who was then critic for *Vanity Fair*) and Guy Bolton recalled that night.

Bolton pointed out to Kern that the man with the large spectacles sitting in the tenth row seemed to be enjoying the show very greatly.

'Wodehouse,' said Kern.

'I suppose it is,' said Bolton. 'But that's only to be expected on an opening night.'

'What on earth are you talking about?'

'You said it's a good house.'

'I didn't. I said Wodehouse.'

And that was how Guy Bolton came to meet P. G. Wodehouse, and how a vital partnership was born.

The final curtain came down to rapturous applause that first night with Mr. Wodehouse cheering as loudly as everyone else. Kern, who had known his one-time collaborator would be in the theatre, approached him after the show. 'What did you think of it?' he asked.

'Not bad at all,' said the man whom everyone seemed to call 'Plum'. 'But the lyrics could be a lot better.' It was not a comment calculated to please Guy Bolton, but he had to admit he preferred to concentrate on the book of his shows and leave the words of the songs to someone else. Together they went back to Jerry's apartment on West 68th Street, where they were soon joined by Laurie and George Grossmith and by Fay Compton, all of whom were currently appearing in *Tonight's the Night* at the Globe Theatre, then being run by Charles Dillingham.

They all knew—and the early morning papers confirmed it—that *Very Good Eddie* was a winner. To celebrate, Jerry played a selection of the show's songs on his piano. His playing was good enough for the guests to enjoy listening to him accompanying members of the cast, and also to him doing a few solo numbers, though he might have found it difficult to sustain an evening at Carnegie Hall. Then he, Bolton and Wodehouse settled down to talk business. In his diary, Bolton recalled that evening: '*Eddie* opened. Excellent reception. All songs hits. To Kern's for supper. Talked with P. G. Wodehouse apparently known as "Plum". Never heard of him, but Jerry says he writes lyrics, so being slightly tight, suggested we team up. Wodehouse, so overcome, couldn't answer for a minute, then grabbed my hand and stammered thanks.'

To judge by their diaries, Guy Bolton and 'Plum' Wodehouse were at different parties—assuming that the notes were written soon after the event. In *his* journal, Wodehouse's memories of the night are slightly at variance: 'Went to opening of *Very Good Eddie*. Enjoyed it in spite of lamentable lyrics. Bolton evidently conscious of his weakness, offered partnership. Tried to hold back and weigh the suggestion, but his eagerness so pathetic that consented. Mem: Am I too impulsive? Fight against this tendency.'

Unfortunately, Jerome Kern kept no diary himself of this momentous event, so perhaps we must accept that the truth lies somewhere between the two recollections. However, it is true that immediately after Bolton and Kern had convinced themselves that *Very Good Eddie* was going to do very good business, they set about establishing the new three-man team, not a usual recipe for success. But they met, talked, scribbled madly and all the time their shows ran, there was never an empty seat at the Princess.

Jerry, meanwhile, was still working on interpolations in other people's shows, and being paid very well indeed for them. To John Golden's lyrics he wrote just one song for the 1916 production, *Go To It*. (Golden did both words and music for the rest of the score.) But the Big Show of 1916 was the year's *Ziegfeld Follies*, for which Jerry contributed so much that it almost deserved to be called the Kern Follies. For a production that featured such magnetic names as Fanny Brice, Bert Williams and Ann Pennington, Kern wrote: 'Have A Heart', 'My Lady Of The Nile', 'When Lights Are Low' and 'Ain't It Funny What A Few Drinks Make?'

He and Eva had decided that the time had come to move away from the noise and grime of the city. They took an apartment at Sagamore Road in Bronxville, then a sleepy, artistic little place in the heart of Westchester County, perhaps two hours drive from the centre of New York City.

For a time, Guy Bolton lived with them. It was a convenient arrangement. 'Plum' Wodehouse would come over from his new bungalow at Bellport, and together they would talk about their next project, a show called *Miss Springtime*. It was something of a complicated arrangement because Bolton and Wodehouse were also working on a musical comedy for the Klaw and Erlanger 'Syndicate'—as sinister an organization as the name implies, because it managed to carve up almost the whole of the American musical and vaudeville theatre to suit its aim of a financial take from everyone's box office. Guy Bolton wrote the book and lyrics for *Miss Springtime* but most of the music was from Emmerich Kalman, with Jerry turning out just three numbers for the show during those Bronxville sessions—'When You're Full Of Talk' and 'My Castle In The Air', for which 'Plum' wrote the lyrics, and 'Saturday Night' with words by Herbert Reynolds.

Despite Eva's earlier insistence, there was no immediate evidence that he had written those pieces in *Miss Springtime*. He himself had asked for his name to be omitted not from any false modesty, or because he thought it was beneath his

44

dignity, but for a much more basic reason. As he told *The New York Times* on January 21, 1917: 'I knew I had several more plays coming on later in the season and I didn't want their chances blasted when they arrived by having some of the critics say that I was trying to do too much—that I was written out. That is such an absurd statement. If one has the gift of melody and a certain amount of intelligence there is no reason why one should not keep on composing good melodies for many years. An author, whose medium of expression is words, keeps on using them in various combinations for many years without the charge of repeating himself or writing himself out, so why should not a composer whose medium is notes keep on making new combinations for them?'

And he made a strange declaration which, had it been anyone but Kern, might be construed as simple modesty: 'I knew that I would get [my name] on the published score and that the names of only two American composers attract people to the theatre—the names of George M. Cohan and Victor Herbert. Except for these, the public doesn't know or care.'

The Times, however, did appear to care about Mr. Kern. His music, the anonymous writer said, 'is melodious, rhythmic and graceful. Not the least of its charms lies in the unfailing daintiness and variety of its orchestration.'

By now, Jerry's life with Eva had settled into a pattern that would remain essentially unchanged for the rest of their lives together. Jerry was the one who wore the pants in the family— very often sail-cloth trousers which he made Eva dye bright green or orange. Guy Bolton told me of his feeling that Eva was being 'put upon' by Jerry and probably she was— although she never stopped loving him, even when considerably depressed about not being able to produce a baby. But Eva was an aloof young woman, and frequently gave the impression of being haughty.

Jerry settled into Bronxville living as though he had been born in a farmhouse and had never asked more of life than a chance to breathe clean country air and spend most of his time talking to the village blacksmith or to the man who kept the corner drugstore. Once the local traders got to know their new neighbour, they called him Jerry. It was while they were in the apartment that Jerry became infatuated with a girl living downstairs. She was beautiful, with a spectacular figure that even Jerry's poor eyesight—he now wore spectacles all the time—managed to appreciate. She was one of a pair of sisters. Whether it was an attempt at some form of subterfuge or simply that he had a bad memory, he would invariably call each girl by the other's name. Eva never suspected any untoward conduct on the part of her husband, even though he would creep downstairs and into the arms of his sweetheart at every opportunity. His great advantage was that he always seemed so sincere in everything he did.

He didn't like to give the impression of being an intense worker. He was too keen on trying to cram as much fun as possible into an evening that rarely began before midnight— even when Eva was far too tired to do anything but go to bed. She still stayed home and Jerry still went to parties.

He never liked very much the idea of driving, but in an age when cars were still rare enough to be regarded as status symbols, he insisted on having one. He—and Bolton and Wodehouse, too for that matter—had reason to be grateful that his car *was* a rarity. Jerry considered the automobile to be principally a vehicle for 'wool-gathering'—a chance to think about anything but the driving. Sitting at the wheel of an open car while the countryside drifted slowly past him was the best way he knew of dreaming up new songs. If other drivers or pedestrians got in his way, that was their problem.

'Plum' Wodehouse had scarcely moved into his Bellport bungalow when Jerry insisted on going along to see the house. It was 'only' 11 o'clock at night when he made the decision to drive with Bolton in the direction of Bellport, which meant that the evening was still young enough for them to arrive by 3 o'clock in the morning. The visit lasted no more than an hour, by which time even Jerry conceded it was getting late and they ought to get back to Bronxville. Halfway home, he fell asleep over the wheel. Fortunately Bolton was able to pull up the handbrake before the large tourer could plunge into a ditch.

Had he not done so, none of them might have been around for the opening of *Miss Springtime* at the New Amsterdam Theatre on September 25, 1916. It was an instant success—so much so that before they could get their first joint Princess show off the ground, Abe Erlanger and Marc Klaw came to them with an offer they could not refuse. The Syndicate—whose official purpose was to put some sort of order into the show business chaos that allowed theatres to double book acts— wanted them to do a show for the Liberty Theatre. Henry Savage would be producing it. It was to be called *Have a Heart* and would star Louise Dresser, Billy B. Van and Flavia Arcaro. It was a highly prestigious deal and one that made the threesome even more in demand than before. Once they were all signed for the Syndicate, Ray Comstock came up with a proposal that was even more tempting. 'Do your Liberty show,' he told them, 'then do another one for the Princess. You can have a contract straight away without my having seen a plot, a synopsis or a script.'

While they considered this next assignment, *Have a Heart* opened at the Liberty on January 11, 1917. Billy B. Van was the sensation of the show—singing a number that Wodehouse had secretly dedicated to Erlanger, a little man with a large Napoleonic complex.

> '*Napoleon was a little guy*
> *They used to call him shorty*
> *He only stood about so high*
> *His chest was under 40.*'

It was not quite the Kern of 'They Didn't Believe Me', but Jerry happily wrote the music and received his share of the fee. One reviewer said of *Have a Heart*, '[It] has the additional asset of a plot—a plot incidentally upon which Mr. Kern's music has always a direct bearing.'

Four days after *Have a Heart* opened, Kern's own show, *Love o' Mike*, for which Harry B. Smith was the lyricist, opened at the Shubert Theatre starring a young dancer called Clifton Webb, two generations later and a different world away to be known as the film character 'Mr. Belvedere'. While *Have a Heart* went on to run for 76 performances, *Love o' Mike* beat it sideways with 192 and songs as forgettable as 'How Was I To Know', 'Moo Cow' and 'Life's A Dance'. All the time, *Very Good Eddie* was still turning away potential patrons—until it reached its 341st performance.

With *Love o' Mike*, Kern himself took control of the orchestrations. He specified, for instance, that there were to be two pianos, a grand and an upright; mandolins and banjos; eight first violins; four violas; two cellos; one bass violin; two flutes; one oboe; one English horn; two bassoons; two trumpets and a set of drums. So with practically no brass to speak of, his music was intentionally playing down the parts of a score that normally are the loudest. When he did use trumpets, he practically neutralized their effect by ordering the players to use mutes.

These were not the only changes he made to the sound of the theatre pit orchestra. He eliminated the second violins because, rightly, he considered they were totally irrelevant to the theatre music of the day—or perhaps he meant the day-after-tomorrow. At the same time, the violas had to work triply hard—serving as rhythm, harmony and melody sections rolled into one. Before long, this new style of orchestration became standardized throughout the whole musical theatre. As a result of Kern's innovations, an orchestra 18–25 strong suddenly found it could do what had previously taken 50 men to accomplish. Musicians protested, but the management over-rode them, and Jerome Kern became a very popular man indeed.

'You, Jerry, are the most unusual composer I've ever worked with,' Henry Savage told him when Kern presented him with his musical requirements. 'But you're not nearly as fussy about your singers. Why don't you insist that your principals should all have good voices?'

'Easy, Henry,' Jerry replied. 'If people really want to hear good singing, they'll go to the opera. In this business, it's much more important to hear the lyrics rendered effectively.' And he went on: 'If he's also a good singer, so much the better. But in our sort of shows, it's much more important if he gets the words over. The orchestra can do the rest.'

He never doubted, of course, that his music was strong enough for the orchestra. The act of composing, for him, still began with a title or a line of lyric which he would then leave until the finished piece of music was handed to his partner. Other composers would see advantages in working with lyricists who were close associates, but he reserved the right to change lyricists whenever it suited him.

He also had plans for the future. He wanted to write a Pierrot-type pantomime. 'I have the idea for it and the offer to

48

produce it,' he said. 'Although the critics will probably jump on me and tell me to go back to my musical comedy tunes, I am going to go through with it.' Like most ambitious men, Kern sometimes allowed himself the luxury of talking about ideas before thinking them out. When he found that critics and managements were cool, he promptly withdrew his toe from the water and thought no more about it.

Oh Boy, the Princess Show which opened on February 20, was a different thing again. It was a smash. But it did not begin that way. The dress rehearsal at Schenectady was a total farce. Everything that could go wrong did go wrong. The early performances were not much better. In the opening stages of *Oh Boy* at Cleveland, the trouble was of a slightly different kind. The show featured established performers like Anna Wheaton, Marie Carroll, Edna May Oliver and two young ladies recently plucked from the *Ziegfeld Follies*—Justine Johnstone and Marion Davies. Marion had had a tiny part in *Very Good Eddie* and was still in the very early days of her association with William Randolph Hearst. The only problem was that Mrs. Jefferson Perry, wife of the company manager and daughter of a leader of Society, considered the presence of two ex-Follies girls to be an affront to her person. They were, she was sure, of a much lower social status. When Guy Bolton introduced them to her, he said: 'You don't know Miss Davies and Miss Johnstone, do you?'

'No,' she replied, 'and I don't care to.'

Such rows are a prescription for disaster in a theatre company, and it didn't help that Mrs. Perry was a friend of Eva Kern. It was 'Plum' Wodehouse's wife, Ethel, who decided she had to make peace in the company and gave a party to achieve just that. Eva arrived for the function wearing a $7,500 pearl necklace that Jerry, confident of the success of *Oh Boy*, had given her, with her friend Mrs. Perry on her arm. The champagne flowed as the guests were served caviar by four waiters. Mrs. Perry was ecstatic—until, that is, she discovered she was at the wrong party. The Wodehouse's beer-and-sandwiches affair was being held upstairs. The one she was attending had been thrown by Miss Davies—subsidized by Mr. Hearst, of course. Mrs. Perry walked off scowling.

In the end, Jerry's premonition of triumph was well founded.

Oh Boy ran for a total of 463 performances—the kind of success that earned *Variety*'s accolade, 'double socco'.

That was precisely the description one could put to the career of Jerome Kern. While *Oh Boy* had followed on *Very Good Eddie*, *Have a Heart* and *Love o' Mike*, with *Miss Springtime* in between, the London theatre was also having a slight attack of Kern fever. Though it was wartime there, the men in khaki and their wives and sweethearts were enjoying his music in shows like *Theodore and Co* and *High Jinks*. As *The New York Times* noted in an essay called 'The Inexhaustible Mr. Kern', 'Outside of these few contributions, Mr. Kern is practically unrepresented on the Anglo-American stage.'

Kern was becoming more and more established as the writer of songs that had a special appeal about them. Nearly all the old German and English influences had left him—if not completely, then certainly to a very considerable extent; although Jerry admitted he was still 'under the spell of Oscar Strauss'. Like Strauss, he took the view that there was more to an orchestra than simply accompanying vocalists or illustrating dancers. It was the orchestra, he said, that provided the atmosphere of a good piece of musical theatre. But his songs were the vital things. And gradually, the important tunes in his life had begun to appear. In *Oh Boy*, the song that mattered was 'Till The Clouds Roll By'. One critic was so impressed with *Oh Boy* that he was inspired to verse:

> *'This is the trio of musical fame*
> *Bolton and Wodehouse and Kern;*
> *Better than anyone else you can name*
> *Bolton and Wodehouse and Kern.*
> *Nobody knows what on earth they've been bitten by,*
> *All I can say is I mean to get lit an' buy*
> *Orchestra seats for the next one that's written by*
> *Bolton and Wodehouse and Kern.'*

It was the biggest stage success of a fairly successful Broadway season. Had there been any doubt before about the kind of revolution that Kern and his two partners had brought off, it was dispelled once the takings at the box office started multiplying like baby rabbits.

The Princess shows were finely tuned to what Marbury and Comstock believed to be the sophisticated New York taste but were also sufficiently American to make touring companies worthwhile. That did not, however, mean they had the same impact overseas. 'The humour of *Very Good Eddie* seems to have been torpedoed in the waist while crossing the Atlantic and much of it failed to get over the footlights at the Palace Theatre,' recorded the *Daily Mail* when the show finally reached London. 'These risky [sic] plays about bedrooms, pyjamas and drink are welcome enough when really amusing and witty. They are hardly so acceptable when, as in the case of this musical comedy, the chief justification for their existence lies in their agreeable trimmings such as music, dresses and dances. The music, by Jerome D. Kern, is almost as melodious as that of *The Belle of New York* which it resembles in rippling variety and ease of expression. It is charmingly sung by Mr. Walter Williams, Miss Madge Saunders and a large and gaily-clad chorus. Mr. Nelson Keys and Mr. Ralph Lynn the comedians make the most of their limited opportunities.'

As for the team, Bolton-Kern-Wodehouse, they had set themselves the target of meeting every commission as it came in and even more important, they had established a working pattern. Wodehouse himself once said that the biggest help to him was to have Kern's music to which he could then add the words—which was, of course, right up Jerry's street, too. 'W. S. Gilbert,' Wodehouse said, 'always said that a lyricist can't do decent stuff that way. But I don't agree with him. I think you get the best results by giving the composer his lead and having the lyricist follow him. For instance, the refrain of one of the songs in *Oh Boy* began: "If every day you bring her diamonds and pearls on a string". I couldn't have thought of that if I had done the lyric first. Why, dash it, it doesn't scan. But Jerry's melody started off with a lot of little twiddly notes, the first thing emphasized being the "di" of diamonds and I just tagged along after him. Another thing is that when you have the melody, you can see which are the musical high spots in it and in fact fit the high spots of the lyric to them. Anyway, that's how I like working and to hell with anyone who says I oughtn't to.'

The influence of the Princess shows on composers and

lyricists was considerable. Lorenz Hart was to say that he played records from the shows all the time—although he was always convinced that he could write better lyrics than Wodehouse.

The success of *Oh Boy* grew more and more stupendous. At one time, there were four companies playing it—three road companies as well as the one at the Princess. It was during the run that Jerry and Guy Bolton had their first real row. They were still living together at Bronxville—which could not always have been the best of arrangements as far as Eva was concerned—on the surface having a marvellous time and drawing four- and sometimes five-figure cheques each from the Comstock management for their trouble. But Bolton thought they were entitled to more.

'Why don't we get in on these shows?' Guy asked Jerry. 'We should each get at least ten per cent.'

Kern replied, 'I don't know if they'll give it to you. Why not talk to them?'

'No,' said Bolton. 'You talk to them. You're a much better businessman than I am.' And indeed, Jerry, who always seemed so self assured, could not dispute it.

The next day, they met again. 'Did you ask him?' Bolton demanded.

'Yes,' Kern replied, 'but they won't do it. They say they can't afford to let 30 per cent out on a show. They've got to give it to the people who are backing them.' As they talked in the empty, dust-sheeted theatre, the pair were interrupted by the company manager who took Jerry aside and handed him a slip of paper.

'What's that?' Bolton asked the manager.

'Oh, nothing,' he replied. 'Just last night's returns.'

'Why didn't you give them to "Plum" and me?' asked Bolton, now growing angry. 'I've seen you give them to Jerry twice.'

'Well,' the manager replied, 'Mr. Kern has ten per cent of the show. You don't.'

As Bolton told me, 'I was really burned up when I heard that.' Comstock and Marbury wanted the team to write another show but Bolton refused. 'I'm not writing with Kern, anymore,' he said, and told Comstock his reasons.

'That's a shame,' the producer said. 'I'm sure you could write a good story.' Bolton, who had by now moved into an apartment of his own on 57th Street and felt no obligation to Jerry, kept repeating: 'It isn't the money. It's the fact that a friend could do this to me.' As he now admits :'Of course, it *was* the money.'

Jerry tried to make peace. 'If you feel like that about it,' he said to Bolton in the smoothest tone he could muster, 'I'll tell you what I'll do. I'll give you half of what I get.' They shook hands on a deal. 'Let's forget it,' said Jerry, smiling kindly.

Bolton told him it was forgotten, but it wasn't. He told 'Plum' about the conversation and his misgivings. 'Of course,' Wodehouse agreed, 'the bastard has cheated us again. He's still got twice as much as we have.' Naturally, Kern wasn't going to allow anything to interfere with his own ten per cent. He had simply found a way of getting Comstock to agree to splitting another ten between the words men. Once more Guy was none too happy with his composer.

Bolton and Wodehouse, however, seemed to get on famously together. 'Guy and I clicked from the start like Damon and Pythias,' Wodehouse wrote. 'Never a harsh word or a dirty look . . . I help him as much as I can with the book end of things but he really does the whole plot. I just do the lyrics, which are easy when one has Jerry to work with.'

But Jerry was never that easy. He was pernickety. If an arranger made a tune sound different from the way in which he had envisaged it, he could be relied upon to tear up the sheet music and order the man to start again—as well as tell him exactly what he thought of him. He particularly hated singers who turned arrangers in their own right. The addition of a single word as a bridge between the two phrases would bring a demand for the vocalist's instant dismissal. 'Those "well singers" make me mad,' he said when a performer turned, for example, 'That's why I love you . . .' into '*Well*, that's why I love you . . .' Already there were people who were calling Mr. Jerome Kern a martinet.

When the triumvirate's show, *Leave It To Jane*, opened at the Longacre Theatre in August 1917, such epithets as 'brilliant' or 'triumphant' were soon exhausted. It was based on George Ade's story *The College Widow*, written twenty years earlier, but the most memorable part was probably the best comedy song Kern had yet produced—'Cleopattera'. The critics, however, seemed to find much more to please them. Charles Danton wrote in the *New York Evening World*: 'Everything at the Longacre Theatre last night was quite up to date. There is no reason to take a great deal of space in saying that the revival of Mr. Ade's frolicsome affair, in fresh guise, is quite as enlivening as it was in its original form. In fact, it gained something last night by way of Mr. Kern's sprightly tunes and by verses that added to the joy of song. You are sure to like *Leave It To Jane*. You needn't leave it to anyone but yourself. A decidedly clever cast makes this assurance doubly sure.'

Guy Bolton had been persuaded, against his better judgement, to do the show with Jerry. He still had not forgiven him, but Comstock was persistent: 'I want to do this show. I've got the money to do it and I want you fellows to write it.' So write it they did and it ran for 167 glorious performances.

Bolton was, nevertheless, induced by Charles Dillingham to cooperate with Kern—and have Wodehouse once more writing the lyrics—in a new show for the Century Theatre. Dillingham, whom Bolton described as 'not the usual Broadway figure at all; a cut above all the others', had a profound knowledge of the theatre that grew out of his love for greasepaint and footlights. The show he was producing now was going to be so big that he even needed Flo Ziegfeld to take some of the production burdens off his shoulders—which meant that it would not stop growing. Not only was Kern writing the music, but Victor Herbert was producing numbers, too, and he normally made it a rule never to co-operate in anything of which he was not in full charge himself. In addition, Ned Weyburn—the man who had taught Fred Astaire how to dance for the stage—was directing the show and the much-acclaimed Joseph Urban was in charge of the sets and costumes, which now played an even more vital part than they had in the Princess productions. Each of the 12 chorus girls had a different costume to wear, and since Wodehouse had to describe—in verse—the ensemble of each, he had a massive 12-verse number to produce.

As usual, Jerry was in on the earliest rehearsals, waiting for that note that would be out of place or a 'well' inserted by

Jerome Kern in 1909, aged 24 years.

*The 'charter' meeting of ASCAP at Luchnows, November 27, 1914.
Kern and Victor Herbert are ringed (right and left, respectively).*

FLORENZ ZIEGFELD

PRESENTS

SHOW BOAT

ADAPTED FROM EDNA FERBER'S NOVEL OF THE SAME NAME

BOOK & LYRICS BY

OSCAR HAMMERSTEIN 2nd

MUSIC BY

JEROME KERN

ENSEMBLES & DANCES BY
SAMMY LEE
SETTINGS BY
JOSEPH URBAN

Make-Believe
Can't Help Lovin' Dat
     Man
Ol' Man River
Why Do I Love You?
Bill
You Are Love
SELECTION

COURTESY
DOUBLEDAY, PAGE & CO.

T. B. HARMS
COMPANY
NEW YORK

The first Magnolia and Gaylord—Norma Terris and Howard Marsh on the stage of the Ziegfeld Theatre on December 27, 1927, when Show Boat was first presented.

(Kobal Collection)

The Cotton Blossom's performers in full steam—from the 1951 film of Show Boat. (Kobal Collection)

Kern and George Gershwin in a recording studio, June 1933.

some poor misguided, unsuspecting soloist. At one early rehearsal, Jerry heard something he didn't like coming from the stage and tore down the aisle, while Dillingham sat in the fifth row of the centre orchestra, obviously quite content with the way things were proceeding. Jerry's face was growing an ever deeper shade of purple. 'Is that how you're going to play my music?' he exploded.

'Yes,' said Dillingham still composed, still the perfect gentleman. 'Yes,' he repeated. 'That's how I'm going to do it.'

A hush descended over the entire auditorium. The rehearsal pianist gradually stopped tinkling the keys, the dancers quietly brought their soft-shoe shuffle to a halt. It was up to Jerry to make the next move. 'In that case,' he replied, 'you can't have it.' He walked down to the footlights and demanded of the orchestra leader: 'Give me that music.' One by one, he collected the sheets from each of the startled musicians in the pit. As he did so, Dillingham's face turned to thunder. 'You'll never enter one of my theatres again,' he roared, pointing in the direction of the nearest exit. 'Never.' Jerry was determined not to lose face, although it seemed he had lost an extremely important fight. With the music secure under his right arm, he stormed out.

The next day, Dillingham sent word to Bronxville. He was sure something could be done to work out a compromise. It could. Kern returned—and his music was played according to the 'authorized version'.

But there were other rows in *Miss 1917* which he did not win. He and Vivienne Segal, for instance, had an unfortunate confrontation. Jerry liked the way Miss Segal sang. He was, in fact, more pleased with her performances than he was with those of Ann Pennington or even Irene Castle. He wanted her to sing one of his songs in the show. Dillingham wanted her to perform a Herbert tune. Since Dillingham was producing, Dillingham won. When Vivienne Segal began singing the song in the dress rehearsal, Jerry stormed towards the stage again.

'You're not singing that,' he said, 'you're singing *my* song.' While Herbert ran down the aisle at the other side of the theatre, shouting, 'No, she's not, she's singing *my* song.'

Eventually Dillingham asked her which tune she preferred. Unfortunately for her relationship with Jerry, she chose

Herbert's number. As a result of that decision, Vivienne was convinced thereafter that Jerry harboured a grudge. (In 1932, she was to try for a part in what looked like being his big hit of the season, *Music in the Air*. He would not even allow her in to audition. She has since said it was a typical example of Kern's vindictiveness. But she did get her revenge. When the show moved to Los Angeles, the role was hers.) *Miss 1917* lasted only 48 performances, but while it ran, it was one of seven Kern shows on Broadway stages during 1917, obviously a very good year for Jerry.

In addition to his own 'Kern' shows, Jerry had written 'Because You're Just You'—with lyrics by Gene Buck—for the 1917 *Ziegfeld Follies*, and two songs (lyrics by Wodehouse) for *The Riviera Girl*, for which Guy Bolton wrote the book.

Naturally, Comstock couldn't wait to get a new Bolton–Wodehouse-Kern show onto the stage—and preferably at the Princess. With *Oh Lady, Lady*, things could not have looked better. Jerry liked the book, loved the settings, and when a new cast list was put before him, did not even raise the slightest objection to the inclusion of Vivienne Segal. The previous disputes with Bolton were now behind him and Kern was left to look after the financial side of the contracts on behalf of his two associates. He settled for ten per cent for himself and $7\frac{1}{2}$ per cent each for Bolton and Wodehouse. He did not, however, have anything to do with the salary of the dark-haired youngster who was sitting in as rehearsal pianist for the company, and whose name was George Gershwin.

Gershwin's job wasn't easy. The rehearsal pianist was paid just $35 a week and in addition to playing for every singer, dancer or acrobat a show might have, he was also expected to be something of a coach. The fact that Gershwin was only 19 did not excuse him from this task. Kern liked the young man. He saw in him something of his own youth—and he also recognized that Gershwin played the piano better than he did.

Only a short while before, Gershwin had attended an aunt's wedding at the Grand Central Hotel in New York. He said later that it was hearing the band play 'They Didn't Believe Me' that had made him decide finally to become a composer himself. 'I followed Kern's work and studied each song he had composed. I paid him the tribute of rank imitation and many things I wrote at this period sounded as though Kern had written them himself.' Gershwin had previously gone to Irving Berlin to ask him for a job as a musical secretary—Berlin could not write music himself and only played the piano in F-sharp, so he had to dictate his tunes. There was a job available, but Berlin told Gershwin that he was much too talented and should move on to other things. He took the advice.

The title of *Oh Lady, Lady* came from the catchphrase of Bert Williams, a Negro artist who was so fair-skinned that he had to use blackface make-up. It had been meant to follow on *Oh Boy*, but the other shows got in the way. Jerry had the feeling that this was going to be one to take off. He and Wodehouse also had a song ready for the show, of which they were really proud. They called it 'Bill'. More accurately, all three of them had a song called 'Bill'. Bolton and Wodehouse had recently come to an agreement by which they shared the royalties on everything they did in the theatre. Wodehouse had half of Bolton's book rights and Bolton half the royalties of Wodehouse's lyrics. They all liked 'Bill', but they all agreed, too, that it had to go. There was just no room for it in the plot. Bill was the name of the juvenile lead, but as a song, it just couldn't be made to fit.

Oh Lady, Lady opened without 'Bill' on its out-of-town try-out in the usual inauspicious circumstances. It was at Wilmington, Delaware, and just three days before Christmas—never a good time to bring patrons into a theatre. The Wednesday afternoon matinee on Christmas Eve was a disaster. The theatre was so empty that the performance might have been a dress rehearsal. Suddenly, from his seat in the middle of the deserted Dupont Theatre, Bolton called out, 'No, Henry, that's wrong. You'll kill the laughs if you keep pointing to that settee . . .' His voice trailed off, as he realized that it was not a rehearsal but a performance for which customers had paid good money. 'Ladies and gentlemen,' he addressed the scattered members of the audience, 'I really must apologize. You were keeping so quiet, I had quite forgotten you were there. I thought we were in rehearsal.'

When the show finally opened at the Princess on February 1, 1918, there was no fear that Broadway audiences would be anything like so subdued. Humorist Dorothy Parker in her guise as a drama critic, wrote: 'Well, Kern, Bolton and Wodehouse have done it again. If you ask me, I will look you fearlessly in the eye and tell you in low, throbbing tones that it has it over any other musical comedy in town. I like the way the action slides casually into the songs. I like the deft rhythms of the song that is always sung in the last act by the two comedians and the comedienne. And oh, how I do like Jerome Kern's music. Every time these three gather together, the Princess Theatre is sold out for months in advance. You can get a seat for *Oh Lady, Lady* somewhere around the middle of August for about the price of one on the stock exchange.'

The show ran for 200 performances at the Princess, and Comstock had no choice but to come to grips with the problem of the limited number of seats at the Princess. The answer was to get a second company simultaneously to play it at the Casino. It was actually not the only additional company. The show was at the same time playing at Sing-Sing—with an all-prisoner cast.

Triumph though it was, *Oh Lady, Lady* was the last of the Princess shows put together by the trio. 'Plum' Wodehouse was anxious to go back to Europe to develop 'Jeeves' and the other multifarious activities that were already making him a very rich man. Guy Bolton was planning a series of shows elsewhere —including one with his rehearsal pianist, George Gershwin— and Jerry was indulging his love of cards and gambling. It sharpened his mind as well as providing him with a great deal of fun. But he saw the other side to it. He once dropped $1,000 in a game. 'It's a poor roulette wheel,' he said after the experience, 'that won't work both ways. It must be the poor ones that I play.' He used to lose so regularly that some of his fellow players ran a book on how much he would go down at the end of an evening at the tables.

The famous columnist of the day, FPA, commented that Kern liked having fun, 'unlike Irving Berlin who really is a sad fellow'. Certainly, he was finding interests as diverse as the inspiration for his songs. Other people had hobbies; Jerry always had passions. When he first saw a signature of Wagner, cut from one of the composer's letters, for sale at an auction he decided that he must collect the autographs of all the great classical composers. And he did—pursuing each one of them with a fervour that sometimes made his composing seem like an interlude in the midst of the searches. From these, he moved to rare books—buying his first for $40 on the advice of his old lyricist partner, Harry B. Smith. But soon he was working very much on his own, collecting books wherever he went, in the second-hand shops of Fifth Avenue and 42nd Street and in London's Charing Cross Road. He was assembling the beginnings of what was to be a vast and valuable library. He not only bought books, but he read them, too. He was also interested to know where they were printed and the method of printing, and all about the paper and the leather used in binding them. It was a serious business that deserved serious consideration.

And so, too, did his home life. Eight years after their marriage, Eva came to Jerry with some important news: 'I'm going,' she said, 'to have a baby.'

We Belong Together

JERRY AND EVA had a new home now, still at Bronxville, but one that was more suited to the status of a man who considered himself the best living popular composer, and was used to hearing himself so described. The three-storey house was at Cedar Knolls. Jerry, his sense of humour keeping pace with his ever-rising station in the music world, called it The Nuts. It was not a big house, although it stood in 10 acres of grounds. But there was room for servants' quarters, a music room and a library, which inevitably became the nerve centre of the whole place, and a spare room which they could now think about turning into a nursery.

Eva desperately wanted a boy. She even had a boy's name ready for the birth—she just would not consider any alternative. Jerry, on the other hand, wanted a girl. On December 16, 1918, as usual it was Jerry's wish that was granted: Elizabeth Jane Kern was born, and from that moment on, Jerry began cultivating not so much a daughter as an idyll. He named the baby after his mother-in-law, which was indeed a singular tribute. His child, he decided, was going to be something special; Elizabeth—or Betty as she was called almost from birth—was going to be his confidante and friend. Eva, on the other hand, was beginning to be regarded by her husband simply as a pleasant companion, certainly not his intellectual equal. When she made a comment that he thought beneath his attention, he would stretch both fists before him and then bring them slowly back—as if pulling pints of beer at The Swan.

The fact that she didn't share his love of parties or of ending the day just as most people were about to begin it, was her loss, he considered. At 1 o'clock in the morning, while she tried to sleep, he would bring a crowd of cronies into the kitchen and collect an armful of the stone crabs of which he was so fond. The guests would be handed hammers and instructed to beat the shells of the crabs, never mind the noise and anyone who might be trying to sleep in the house. Jerry expected to be left to sleep until noon, but poor Eva had to get up at six to feed Betty. Guests at The Nuts had to fit into Jerry's pattern of living. He expected a full breakfast at a time when no one else was ready to eat, and then wouldn't want dinner until very late in the evening.

Against the background of this eccentric routine, he and Guy Bolton were once more planning a new show. Bolton remembers spending most of the day slumped in an arm chair: 'I couldn't move around because Jerry wasn't planning dinner until late and I needed sustenance so badly.'

Jerry's wife, however, needed something more. 'I always felt she led a pretty dull life,' recalls Bolton. 'I don't ever remember seeing her smile. She never laughed. She was never gay. She always looked as though she was worried about something. She had a rather hang-dog expression.' He thinks it was 'unfortunate for her' that she married Jerry. But he has no doubt that she loved him. If she had any thoughts about looking after Betty herself—and theirs was by now an upper middle-class English style home, so it is quite possible that she did not—Jerry disabused her of the notion. No, his daughter would have the finest nurse that money could buy.

As far as *The New York Times* was concerned, his professional position was assured: 'It is necessary periodically,' it stated in 1918 in a piece headed 'Kern the Industrious', 'to stand still for a moment and gaze upon the labours to date of one Jerome Kern. In the old days, Kern generally had to content himself with sneaking a single melody into the score of some Viennese composer. Generally, the Kern melody was the hit of the piece and invariably the foreign composer got the credit for it. Now, however, things are different and it was not altogether the war which has brought the change. Ability and industry will out and at 33 Kern finds himself today one of the successful and sought after composers of the world ... Certainly, no other American composer can point to so many New York productions in a single season.' (There had been five *new* Kern shows the previous year and six in 1918.) 'If the Kern scale of mathematical progression holds, there will be seven Kern shows on Broadway next season and eight the season after that. If he lives to be 70, there is no telling what may happen.'

The magazine *Musical Courier* was equally amazed by Kern's prodigious output. He was, said the paper at the time when his show *Head Over Heels* opened at the Cohan Theatre, 'the most popular and prolific composer of light opera music today'. It pointed out that he was the son of an Irish Jew—and if that was not strictly accurate, nor was their next statement: 'Writing the numbers of a musical comedy is no more of an effort for Kern than writing a letter. His extraordinary facility is proved by the great number of pieces to his credit this last season and by the prodigious amount of work he has done on scores that never bore his name at all.'

It was true to say that inspiration did come frequently and fairly easily to Kern. But that was not the same as suggesting that it took no effort. Once the idea had been born, he spent hours developing and then perfecting his creations. Kern, however, did say that it was sometimes easier to dash off a musical comedy score than it was to figure out how much might be coming to him in weekly royalties. And in 1918, that was frequently in the region of $5,000. Such an income put Jerome Kern, even at that young age, among the top composers in America.

When Gershwin had worked for him as rehearsal pianist, Kern had told him that he knew the young man would one day write a show of his own. 'And when you do,' he said, 'come to me and I'll help you with it.' That show came earlier than either could have imagined, in 1919. Gershwin's producer, Alex Aarons, advised George to ignore the offer—he would be better off working it out for himself. When Jerry got to hear of this, soon after the opening of that first big Gershwin show, *La La Lucille*, he was so furious with Gershwin that he vowed never to speak to him again. His silence lasted for the best part of three years.

The Cohan Theatre, incidentally, was becoming as much Kern's 'home' theatre as had been the Princess. *Head Over Heels* followed his own army musical, *Toot Toot*, there. It was based on the Rupert Hughes' story *Excuse Me*, and lasted a mere 40 performances. *Head Over Heels* was more successful. It ran for 100 performances. *Rockabye Baby*, which was the last Kern show of 1918, survived for 85—with the help of a cast list that included Frank Morgan and Louise Dresser.

He also interpolated three songs in *The Canary*, a show for which P. G. Wodehouse had written the lyrics. But, strange though it seems, two of Kern's tunes, 'Take A Chance Little Girl' and 'Learn To Dance', had words by Harry B. Smith, and the lyrics for the third, 'Oh Promise Me You'll Write Him Today', were by Edward Clarke.

In 1919, Jerry was back in London, where, still as much at home as he had been before the war, he was working on a show called *Oh Joy!* starring the darling of the West End stage, Beatrice Lillie. It was about a young man who tries to hide the fact that he has just become married. Said the *Daily Mail*: '*Oh Joy!* is as racy as the average bedroom piece of the moment and equally inoffensive. Its greatest charm is Jerome Kern's sparkling music. Mr. Kern's score is full of catchy, exhilarating melodies; one of them especially, "When The Rain Comes Pitter-Patter", will soon be heard in every drawing-room.'

It was still important for Jerry to write shows specifically for the London stage—like *The Cabaret Girl*, which took him a week to produce, with lyrics by Wodehouse. It was not Kern's most brilliant score, but it did well enough to cross the Atlantic. 'After two postponements,' recorded the *Daily Express*, '*The Cabaret Girl* was produced at the Winter Garden Theatre on Tuesday and she was worth waiting for. Mr. George Grossmith and Mr. P. G. Wodehouse have not only been singularly happy in their collaboration as authors; they have also been lucky in their composer. Mr. Jerome Kern's light music sparkles with tuneful lightness.' The papers seem to have been greatly impressed both with Dorothy Dickson's charm and the dramatic abilities of George Grossmith and Norman Griffin, to say nothing of the pretty girls and their dresses.

63

The Cabaret Girl was followed soon afterwards by *The Beauty Prize*, starring Heather Thatcher. The London *Daily Express* said of *The Beauty Prize*: 'It is quite as smart and still more inane than most entertainments of its type. As for Jerome Kern's tunes, if they fall below the level of *The Cabaret Girl*, one or two of them will (and should) soon be all over the ballrooms.' The paper noted that there appeared to be a 'division of opinion in the gallery when the final curtain fell, but the "ayes" were in the majority and cheers overwhelmed any discontented sounds. There was a special call for Miss Heather Thatcher.'

He was as much at home in London as ever. 'What, Mr. Kern,' he was asked one night at a dinner party, 'would you say was the chief characteristic of the American nation?'

'The American,' Kern replied, 'is epitomized in Irving Berlin's music, in that both of them have humour, originality, pace and popularity. Both are wide awake and both sometimes are a little loud. But what makes both unsympathetically be mistaken for brass is really gold.'

There is no doubt that Kern had the profoundest respect for Berlin's work. 'Irving Berlin,' he said, 'has no place in American music. He *is* American music.' And since he considered himself Berlin's rival, it was generosity indeed.

Back home in the States, the mathematical progression forecast by *The New York Times* was broken. There was only one wholly Kern show on Broadway, *She's a Good Fellow* at Dillingham's Globe Theatre. But the list of productions in which he interpolated songs included *Zip Goes a Million*, *Charm School* and *The Lady in Red*.

The following year was much more productive. It began with *Night Boat* (which Richard Rodgers was to say had a 'delectable score'), with songs like 'Some Fine Day', 'Who's Baby Are You' and 'A Heart For Sale'. *Hitchy Koo of 1920* followed, a revue featuring a young soprano called Grace Moore. Charles Dillingham produced the show and the real stars were Raymond Hitchcock and the lovely Julia Sanderson. But Jerry was struck with both the beauty and the voice of young Miss Moore. He wanted her to sing his favourite number of the show, 'The Wedding Cake', for which she would wear a superb bridal gown and sit atop a cake covering the entire width of the stage.

For the very ambitious and very pretty Grace Moore, it was the fulfilment of all her dreams—until Julia Sanderson decided that she wanted the song for herself, and Grace had to content herself with singing 'Moon of Love', while 12 beautiful chorus girls recited against her melody, 'What the hell do we care about the moon of love, above?' Yet it was Miss Moore who was noticed more than anyone else that first night at the New Amsterdam Theatre on October 21, 1920. In one scene, she was waltzing with Raymond Hitchcock when from beneath her long hooped gown appeared a pair of panties. All she could do was stoop down, gather them into a bundle and finish her dance while the audience and the rest of the cast roared. From that night on, she was known as 'The Girl Who Lost Her Pants'. However, she managed to live it down and later made a number of notable films and sang a song for which she would always be remembered, 'One Night Of Love', before dying tragically young in an air crash.

The show itself was most notable for its music. But, good as it was, nothing in the Kern story to date compared with what came next—a new show with Guy Bolton, which Florenz Ziegfeld was producing at the New Amsterdam Theatre. That fact alone was sufficient to guarantee a spectacular—but not even Ziegfeld had had a success like *Sally*, a show that had every imaginable Ziegfeld touch, all of them adding up to extravagance. One of these touches was to retain two composers and three lyric writers, with Guy Bolton in charge of the book. Not content with employing Kern to write the score, he prevailed on Victor Herbert to provide a suite of ballet music. The two men stuck closely to their own particular fields, but the lyricists created problems and involved Jerry in a series of scenes with the third member of the former Princess team, 'Plum' Wodehouse.

'Plum' had talked about *Sally* to both Bolton and Kern and fondly believed that this was going to be another opportunity for the old partnership. He happily sent over two lyrics for Kern's attention—'Joan Of Arc' and 'The Little Church Around The Corner', only to learn that Ziegfeld had retained Clifford Grey and Buddy De Sylva as lyricists. 'Plum' immediately cabled Kern withdrawing his lyrics from the show. Jerry was predictable. He sent him a telegram, 'the sort of cable', Wodehouse reported afterwards to his stepdaughter Leonore, 'that the Kaiser might have sent to an underling'. Jerry maintained that Wodehouse's action in withdrawing the lyrics was 'extremely offensive' and ended his wire: 'YOU HAVE OFFENDED ME FOR THE LAST TIME.'

Kern took it a stage further. He began an action against Wodehouse demanding payment of royalties on *Miss Springtime* and *Riviera Girl* which he claimed to be owed. 'Plum' remarked at the time: 'Of course, he hasn't an earthly and I don't suppose the action will ever come to anything, but doesn't that show how blighted some blighters can be when they decide to be blighters?' As things turned out, there was no action, and Wodehouse and Kern once more became friends and were to collaborate again.

But Jerry was not the sort of man to be tangled with thoughtlessly. Once he had an idea in his head, it was not easily dislodged. Not even the great Ziegfeld could persuade Jerry to part with his song 'Bill' so that it could be used in *Sally*, for he was still determined that a song should fit the plot and he could see no way of 'Bill' becoming part of *Sally*. Ziegfeld had been introduced to the tune on a pre-show cruise on The Wench, a yacht he had hired partly as a means of relaxing tensions among the *Sally* crew and partly as an opportunity to court Marilyn Miller. He had decided that Marilyn would be better than Ruth Etting in the role of the girl from the orphanage employed to wash up in a fashionable restaurant. As Kern played the 'Bill' melody, Ethel Petit, who had starred in *Miss Springtime*, sang it.

'I've got to have that song,' Ziegfeld said.

'It's not for sale,' said Jerry. 'It's a valuable adjunct for a show.'

'We'll use it in *Sally*,' replied Ziegfeld

'You can't,' Kern replied firmly. 'It won't fit.'

'I want it for the *Follies*,' Ziegfeld countered, regardless. 'I'll have Fanny Brice sing it. She's ideal for the song. She'll give it a big send up with plenty of schmaltz.'

But Jerry was determined that 'Bill' would not be wasted. He wanted it for a book show, and schmaltz didn't come into it. *Sally* was just not *the* show.

They did not disagree about everything. Both wanted the opening number of *Sally* to be so opulent the audience's eyes would pop and stay popping all evening. Guy Bolton and Marilyn Miller however, didn't want that sort of beginning. They saw the opening as a parade of six orphan girls, all dressed alike in gingham, waiting to be inspected by a restaurateur searching for the dishwasher who was to be at the centre of the show. This wasn't glamorous enough for Ziegfeld. It didn't provide the big opening number that Kern wanted, but Bolton proved the more forceful, and the orphan girls won. But apart from that number and the scene in which Marilyn Miller sang, surrounded by a mountain of dirty dishes, Kern's 'Look for the Silver Lining', opulent the show was. As for the 'Silver Lining' number, it was to far outdistance the show from which it came and it, too, is now a standard.

Miss Miller's salary was said to be $3,000 a week, plus a percentage of Ziegfeld's gross—a figure never previously topped on Broadway. *Sally* had an equally unusual position in the story of the American theatre because it ran for 570 performances. It also really marked the end of a time when Kern was happiest writing for small, intimate shows. *Sally* was big, and he enjoyed being hailed as a Big Songwriter to go with it.

Not everyone, however, was impressed with Jerry. Fred Fisher, one of the most successful songwriters of the period, who had written outstanding songs like 'Chicago', 'Peg O' My Heart', and that paean to parenthood, 'Daddy You've Been A Mother To Me', thought he recognized something familiar about Jerry's 'Ka-Lu-A' when his 1921 show, *Good Morning Dearie* opened at the Globe. A recurring bass note, he declared was identical to one in his own recent hit 'Darenella'. Jerry claimed to be affronted. 'I never plagiarize anything,' he declared drawing himself up to his full 5 feet 6 inches. But his protests did not appease Fisher, who promptly sued for $1 million in damages. Kern mustered his own legal forces. It was, said his lawyer, a device used in 'the works of the masters, more or less ancient'. And to prove his point, pianos were moved into a room adjoining the court, and professional musicians demonstrated Kern's theories. Leopold Stokowski gave supporting evidence. A similar refrain *had* been used time and time again

67

in classical music, he said. Fred Fisher seemed to be beaten. In a break in the court proceedings, he went up to Kern. 'Tell you what, Jerry,' he said, 'I'll settle for a new suit like yours.'

Jerry, as immaculate as ever, with the cuffs of his jacket tightly fastened with buttons (so that they could be rolled back when he was working) and with a long Liberty silk scarf folded around his neck in place of the conventional tie, bristled. 'You will get no such thing,' he said, and stormed off to a conference with his lawyer.

The case proceeded, and to every question from the plaintiff's attorney and each aside from the judge, Kern had a truculent answer. As the hearing wore on, so Jerry's temper wore out. Finally, the judge, who had privately doubted whether there could be any case to bring against Kern, decided against him. His decision, he said, was very firmly based on Jerry's uncooperative stance. He awarded the lowest amount of damages that the law then recognized—$250.

Despite it all, *Good Morning Dearie* had a respectable run of 265 performances. Certainly, it was no *Sally*, although perhaps it could be argued that these were strange times. For weeks, the attention of Americans had been diverted by a bill pending in the State legislature of Utah threatening fines and imprisonment for any woman who wore her skirt more than three inches above the ankle, and by another in Virginia banning the exposure of more than three inches of throat. Fictional Broadway stories could hardly compete with actual situations like these.

But *Sally* was more than big enough to carry the name Jerome Kern over this small hurdle. It made the customary provincial and overseas tour, and was acclaimed wherever it went. Its London reception, however, was slightly mixed. The *Sunday Express* reported: 'A new American musical comedy, *Sally*, had a fine reception at the Winter Garden Theatre last night. Except for a few boos, which were instantly drowned in applause, and for a single admonition from the gallery to "hurry up" when the action began to drag, it was "roses all the way".' The paper said that few shows were more lavishly staged than *Sally*. 'Its scenery and dresses and the tuneful music of Jerome Kern are almost sufficient in themselves to ensure success. The costumes in the Butterfly Ballet were so novel and beautiful that each one, as it appeared, was greeted with rounds of applause. The production, however, is reminiscent in every detail. It is the old Cinderella story to which American musical comedy producers appear to be chained for life. Much of the humour seems to have been lost in crossing the Atlantic and Mr. Leslie Henson had to work very hard to infuse life into the so-called "dialogue". Miss Dorothy Dickson, the Sally, is an excellent dancer, but an indifferent vocalist and actress.'

The *Daily Mail*, too, described Kern's music as 'reminiscent', but it was also 'delicious' and 'survives the ordeal of transportation'.

As though to prove how unpredictable the success story of a songwriter of even Jerome Kern's stature could be, his next show was much less of a triumph—although worse was still to come. Neither Charles Dillingham's production nor the exuberant presence of the brilliant young dance team of Fred and Adele Astaire in one of their earliest Broadway shows, could prevent *The Bunch and Judy* from going under. Fred Astaire told me: 'It was a flop show. It didn't deserve to do any better. There wasn't very much good music, either. It was one of those things you go through and try to forget as fast as you can.'

The show opened at the Globe on November 28, 1922, and lasted for just three weeks. The Astaires sang 'How Do You Do, Katinka' but the public just did not want to know, although the critics appear to have loved it. Percy Hammond said: 'We do not recall anything recent in a musical comedy quite so entertaining as *The Bunch and Judy*. It has all the merits possible to exercises of its type.' And Kenneth McGowan wrote: '*The Bunch and Judy* luxuriates. There will be no other show in that theatre this year.' He was just about right; there was only one week of the year to go when it closed.

It was a disappointment for Jerry, but not a strong enough one to make him think of taking up another occupation. He did, after all, have another show on which to work. And as usual, he was planning to take Eva to London, although it was not simply *her* entertainment he was considering.

In London, they took large rooms at Claridges and Jerry was feted by the musical fraternity and entertained by leading figures in café society who now nightly danced away the small hours to Jerome Kern's music. The Prince of Wales, trend-setter par excellence, asked him to a party. 'I don't think you'd enjoy it at all,' Jerry told Eva, 'why not go and visit with your family?' So Eva went to Walton and Jerry met the Prince of Wales. In truth, she was probably a lot happier at the Swan, while Jerry was ecstatically playing 'Look For The Silver Lining' for the Prince, and explaining to him how he managed to get bright green trousers to wear for less formal moments at home.

Eva was certainly happiest in New York, a city she had come to love. She might have loved her life there even more if Jerry had been just a little more considerate. It sometimes happened that, at the end of an evening dining with friends, having kissed his hostess on the cheek and guided Eva to the elevator outside the apartment, Jerry would turn into someone very different from his sophisticated reputation. If there were other people in the elevator, a glint would come into his eye and he would start to shout, 'I tell you, good people, drink is evil and you must fight it. The demon will come and get you.' Meanwhile, Eva would stand cowering in the corner, desperately trying to dissociate herself from this maniac temperance lecturer. Outside in the street, Jerry would call for his car and with a polite, 'Come, my dear', open the door for her. 'Very pleasant evening, wasn't it?' he would remark, with no reference to the practical joke he had just perpetrated.

Hardly surprisingly, his sense of humour was generally more appreciated by their friends than by Eva. Even the servants enjoyed 'Mistah Jerry's' little jokes. In fact, they appreciated most things about him. If in the theatre Kern had a reputation for being a martinet, at home he treated his servants kindly and fairly. Too kindly, thought Eva. Having been brought up in the hotel business, she thought she knew how to direct staff. It was the one way in which she felt she had an advantage over her husband. But Jerry wouldn't listen to her. The only time he complained about the servants was when the cooking slipped below gourmet standards, and that was rare indeed.

He was as devoted to watching ballgames as he was to cards and to collecting books. Every Saturday he would go to the games with Max Dreyfus. 'If an outfielder muffed a flyball,

Jerry would go crazy,' Dreyfus recalled. 'He really could lose his temper.' The ballgames were also an opportunity for him to discuss business with Dreyfus, with whom he had become partner in the Harms publishing firm.

The money he was now earning enabled Jerry to indulge his most extravagant and absurd whims. For instance, one day, glancing out of his bedroom window, he noticed that the grass had grown around the house to a seemingly unmanageable height. He decided that the solution to this was to buy a flock of sheep. The only trouble was that at lambing time the whole house and all the neighbours were kept awake at night. He worried about the animals and their welfare, and finally decided that they would have to go.

Although he teased Eva unmercifully and, at times, seemed a hard man both to her and to his business associates, he did have his endearing side. A girl in the cast of one of his shows who sang particularly well would receive from him a single rose. A courteous doorman would be given a theatre ticket. 'He was always so graceful to his friends,' one of them remarked many years later.

However, he did have an impish desire to make Eva feel uncomfortable—not because he disliked her, simply because he found her reactions so very funny. It was cruel of him to make her use the telephone, an instrument which in the early years of their marriage absolutely terrified her. 'Evalina,' he would call, using the extended form of her name which he also found funny, 'the telephone is ringing.' He refused to answer it himself, and would also make her call people up for him. When the maid or butler answered a ring and called Jerry to the phone, he would insist instead that Eva take the call and write down a message for him. He didn't mind talking on the phone, but usually left it to a secretary or one of the servants. It saved him from being involved in unnecessary conversations—although that was not why he made Eva use it. He quite clearly enjoyed seeing her discomfort. It was a good joke.

Yet, in his way, he loved Eva, though the love he showed her was nothing compared to the adoration he felt for Betty. When the time came for her to go to school, Jerry decided that it was necessary for her to see something of the less privileged world outside. Instead of sending her to an expensive private school, he enrolled her at the local Bronxville public school, to which she was taken each day by her nurse, who would collect her at the end of the afternoon. The other children teased her mercilessly about her fine clothes and the excesses of her rich parents, and today she says she would have been much happier in a private school where she would not have stuck out like a sore thumb, but Jerry couldn't understand that. He wanted her to mix with the neighbours' kids, but saw no reason why she should dress or behave like them.

For a time now, Jerry seriously contemplated retirement. He even told George Gershwin that he would present him with his unfulfilled show contracts, which, considering that three years before Jerry had felt the young man had snubbed him, was tribute indeed. However, Kern continued to work and Gershwin—without too much trouble—found his own contracts.

People used to remark on Jerry's 'nervous energy' and it is true he set himself and others impossibly high standards; but generally the results were worth the efforts. He usually looked more fierce than he really was. His head was slightly cocked to the left—as the years went on the angle grew more acute—due probably to a malformation of the spine. One famous lyricist tells the story of the time he talked to Jerry about the number on which they were collaborating. Jerry, head on side, was pensive. Until, that is, the lyricist mentioned the percentage of the royalties he wanted. Jerry's head, he says, suddenly shot up, quite erect. But this is the only suggestion that Kern's posture was an affectation rather than an affliction.

Kern could, however, affect moods, and so, he believed, could the face of Wagner, a six-inch-high bronze bust of whom stood, together with one of Mozart, on the piano as he worked. As Jerry finished playing a new number, so he would glance in the direction of Wagner. 'He liked it,' he'd say, hugging Eva or Betty after a successful afternoon's work. 'Wagner smiled at me.' He was equally convinced that if Wagner did not approve, the bronze face would scowl in his direction.

Wagner must have liked *Stepping Stones*, the 1923 show at the Globe Theatre that Jerry wrote with Anne Caldwell, one of only two really successful women lyric writers then at work in America. The show—with numbers like 'In Love With Love' and 'Dear Little Peter Pan' as well as the title tune—ran for

241 performances.

How Wagner reacted to the score that Jerry turned out for a show called *Sitting Pretty* is not so easy to imagine. The show opened at the Fulton Theatre on April 8, 1924, intended as a reprise of the Princess productions—once, that is, Irving Berlin was out of the way. Ray Comstock and Maurice Gest had had an idea for a show; Guy Bolton was to write the book and Berlin the score. It would star the extremely popular Duncan Sisters. However, the sisters had an offer they considered more attractive in the title roles of a musical based on *Uncle Tom's Cabin* called *Topsy and Eva*. It was a tremendous hit, and they dropped out of the Comstock show. When Berlin realized they were not going to do it, he withdrew too, and Jerry was brought in to replace him. Wodehouse and Bolton were asked to do lyrics and book.

Wodehouse wrote at the time: '[Kern] has done a fine score but it still remains to be seen whether or not the show written as a vehicle for a sister act, will succeed with its present cast. We have Gertrude Bryan and Queenie Smith for the two Duncan parts and they are both good but in my opinion they aren't a team and this may dish it. A pity if that happens as it is really a good show.' As things turned out, Wodehouse's forebodings were correct, and Irving Berlin, who had an uncanny instinct for knowing whether he should do things or not, was right to turn down the show. The 60-odd performances for which *Sitting Pretty* ran made it the only Princess show not to complete a New York season.

It is possible that there was another reason for the flop of *Sitting Pretty*. Jerry had taken it into his head to be extremely difficult about the show's music being played outside the theatre, and in fact imposed a total ban on it being played in cabarets, on records and also on the flourishing new medium, the radio. He also insisted above all that it should never be played by a jazz band. In his perverse way, Jerry was trying to make a point. What he did not realize was that a colossal proportion of ticket-buying patrons now went to see a show simply because they had already heard and liked the music. Jerry, however, firmly believed that music should be played as the composer had intended it to sound. 'It is about time,' he pronounced, 'that someone should take a stand against the maltreatment of music by the average jazz orchestra. Jazz is not a style of performing music. It is a degradation of style. What is the use of asking a jazz orchestra to play any piece of music nowadays? They make them all sound alike when they get hold of them. The star performer in a jazz orchestra gets $200 a week, not because he is a good player but because he can pervert melodies more ingeniously than the next man. These people are responsible for the fact that playing popular tunes in the home is as dead as bicycle riding.'

It must be said, of course, that the 'jazz' he was talking about was not the kind that any jazz afficionado would today recognize. It was a forerunner of swing in which band arrangers would improvise too much for Kern's taste. While other songwriters shrugged their shoulders and waited for the royalty cheques, Kern would jump in the air and shout: 'My God, just listen to what they have done to the burthen of my song.'

He even insisted that ASCAP should refuse to license the *Sitting Pretty* music. 'That may mean that they'll throw me out,' he said, 'but I hope not. Because what we're doing here is more important than the money the society would collect each year in royalties. It is something for the future of American light music which today has no chance whatsoever and is mere barbaric mouthing.'

Was he really serious about banning his music from the radio? If the newspapers could be believed, people were falling over themselves to buy crystal-sets. In New York, they were being installed in the swish penthouses overlooking Central Park and in the tenement blocks on either side of the street markets of the Lower East Side. By banning radio performances of his *Sitting Pretty* music, he seemed to be cutting off his nose to spite his face. 'I have no objection to broadcasting music if it is transmitted directly from the theatre where it will be rendered by trained artists,' he said. 'But no jazz orchestras.'

A mere sixty-two performances proved that Jerome David Kern sometimes made mistakes.

I'll Be Hard to Handle

KERN'S MUSIC, said one writer, affected the American masses in much the same way as the arias of grand opera had appealed to the citizens of Milan a hundred years before. It was no more than the truth. The sophisticated Kern tunes were not only being played and sung and danced to in theatres and ballrooms on both sides of the Atlantic—his views about jazz apart—but were being whistled and hummed in the streets. He had bridged two worlds and in doing so had virtually created a new kind of pop music, melodic enough to satisfy his own standards, relevant to the action of a play, yet catchy enough to appeal to people who had never been inside a theatre in their lives.

Firmly convinced of his own superiority, Kern could afford to be generous about others in the music writing business. When a tune came into the Harms office that he liked, he would take it home, play it and then generally give the impression that he wished he had thought of it first. Of his contemporaries, he said: 'Vincent Youmans is the best for melodies, George Gershwin the best for rhythm, and for an out and out song writer there is no one to touch Irving Berlin.' Needless to say, in each case he meant 'after me'.

Jerry was always keen to share his enthusiasm for what he had produced. If, as he sometimes did, he finished a new number while sitting at a battered upright piano at the corner of a stage, he would summon anyone within earshot—producer, lyricist, call boy, scenery shifters—to come and listen. If, on the other hand, a number did not come out the way he wanted it, the lid would be slammed down over the piano keys and Jerry's language would rival that of a sailor who has just been over-charged for a tot of rum.

He prided himself on being quick on the uptake, and did not take kindly to being taken advantage of. But he also knew when not to complain. Once, drawn into an antiquarian bookstore by the sight of a first edition that he had badly wanted for a long time, he was quite well aware that the shop manager was engaging him in conversation while one of his assistants trebled the price on the volume. Jerry knew the exact market price of the book because he had researched it, but as far as he was concerned, it was worth ten times the marked-up price. He paid without demur. Often, however, he returned volumes sent to him on approval with an angry note to the dealer, who either knew less than he did himself or was quite clearly trying to cheat him. Jerry said at that time, 'I have returned more books sent to me on approval by foreign dealers than I have bought. Foreigners seem more interested in the titles of books while the American dealer stresses the condition of preservation.'

Occasionally dealers told him he was paying excessive prices. He usually pretended it did not matter; in any case he was far too astute a businessman ever to be pressured into buying an item he did not really want. There were times when he had to suffer the indignity of being laughed at in an auction room after bidding further than any professional dealer or collector was willing to go. But he wasn't buying the books for financial investment and there was no thought in his mind at that stage of ever selling his collection. Meanwhile, it had become a popular talking point at those Kern dinner parties, which Jerry would dominate with his wit.

Sometimes, he could use that wit to end abruptly a conversation he did not think worth pursuing. Like the time a procession of cars stopped outside their next-door neighbours' house. 'Oh,' asked Eva, 'are the Jacksons entertaining?' 'Not very,' replied Jerry, going over to the piano and starting to toy with the idea for a new song. Another time, Eva went to the window remarking, 'I wonder if it is going to rain.' Jerry did not answer. 'I said,' she repeated, 'I wonder if it is going to rain.

You didn't say anything.'

'I didn't say anything,' Jerry finally answered crushingly, 'because "I wonder if it is going to rain" is a statement not a question.'

His attitude to lyric writers was likely to be equally abrupt if he thought their work had not been done to the best of their ability. On the other hand, if a lyricist produced a lyric he did like, it would be greeted with all the excitement of a child given a birthday present. He would play it joyfully, with eyes closed, shouting the words like a Salvationist pouring out hymns. He never pretended to be a lyricist, but nearly always he would scribble a dummy lyric before handing a bundle of manuscript paper to the man who was actually going to write the words. Usually, his verse had about it all the poetry of 'Little Bo Peep' and none of the lasting quality, but it gave the flavour of what he had in mind, and when he sang it—sometimes over the telephone—to his lyricist it was as though he were reciting the work of Shelley or Wordsworth.

More than one lyricist was to complain about being handed a bundle of manuscript paper with the instruction from Jerry: 'The one on the top is the comedy song.' He was, hardly surprisingly, not the easiest partner for a lyric writer to work with. His ideas were too formulated to allow others the kind of artistic licence he expected for himself. He liked 'well' lyricists no more than he appreciated 'well' singers, and when asked for a 'grace note'—a link between two phrases—if he didn't feel like writing one, the lyricist just had to manage without. The mere mention of his name was sufficient to strike fear into the hearts of many young writers.

Impresarios frequently had a similar reaction. Philip Goodman, a man who had spent his entire working career in advertising, fancied himself as a theatre manager and approached Kern to write a show for him. When they first met, Jerry sized up the man before him: 'Good morning, Mr. Goodman,' he said. 'I'm Kern. I hear you're a son-of-a-bitch. So am I.'

Son-of-a-bitch he might be, but Goodman also loved the theatre and unlike many managers, appreciated the value of quality. He had heard about a young man called Howard Dietz who wrote the kind of verses that made good lyrics.

Jerry, who was always ready to give new talent a try, agreed to think about letting Dietz work with him on the Goodman show. In his book *Dancing In The Dark*, Dietz describes getting a call from Kern which went as follows: 'Is that Howard Dietz, otherwise known as Freckles? This is Jerry Kern and I'm a fan of yours.'

Dietz couldn't believe it really was Kern. 'Take a chance on it,' Jerry replied. 'Is that really the author of "I've A Bungalow In Babylon On Great South Bay"?'

'Yes, Mr. Kern,' he replied, adding, 'I know by heart every song you and Mr. Wodehouse ever wrote and I think I'm going to faint.'

Kern persuaded him not to faint and to consider a deal. 'Come up to Bronxville tomorrow,' he said, 'and we'll go over the whole thing. Take the 11.22 train and get a taxi to the station. Charge the taxi to me.' True to his word, Jerry paid for the taxi and received Dietz in his ever-growing library. 'It was hard to imagine musical trivialities born in this atmosphere,' he records in his book. Jerry might have been only 5 feet 6 inches tall but at that moment he was a 'giant ornamented with gold braid'.

Kern was planning not only to create new numbers to which Dietz could put the words, but also to use some of the old songs he had written for English musicals that had never come off. The show was to be called *Dear Sir*—about a charity ball where the principal prize in the evening's auction would be the most beautiful girl on the floor. 'This might be the opening chorus,' he said, handing Dietz one of the manuscript sheets. 'This might be called the icebreaker.' The papers piled up in Dietz's outstretched arms as Kern continued his running commentary: 'This is the love scene, this is a comedy duet, this is a useful jingle which could be used as a finale . . .'

It was Wednesday. Did Dietz think he could produce something worthwhile by Friday? He said he could—not sure whether he was bluffing himself more than he was trying to convince Kern. He turned down the offer of a cup of tea because he was too nervous to accept it, and was ushered out of the house, papers falling from his arms like tumbling snow.

All day and all night, Dietz worked. By the time Friday came, he was punch drunk from his labours. But there was a lyric for every tune, and as he hummed them to himself in the train out to Bronxville that morning, they didn't sound at all bad. Kern asked him pleasantly if he had managed to do any work. 'Yes,' Dietz said and produced the first sheet of lyricized music.

'You've finished *one*?' Jerry said, brimful of excitement. 'I don't believe it!'

The lyrics he had written to a comedy song delighted Kern. It was a twist on the verse by Noël Coward, 'If You Will Be My Morganatic Wife'—which Jerry had scribbled on the top of the sheet to give Dietz the rhythm of the song he wanted. Dietz made it 'If We Could Lead A Merry Mormon Life'. When he had finished playing the tune and stopped singing the words to himself, Kern told Dietz: 'That number alone will make the score great.'

Dietz travelled home to Manhattan feeling as though he were walking on air. As he pranced down the hallway of his apartment block, he shouted: 'I've conquered Kern!'

He had, however, not conquered Broadway. *Dear Sir*, starring Walter Catlett and Genevieve Tobin, lasted for just fifteen performances. It took more than that, though, to dim Kern's enthusiasm. Swear he might, but he refused to get depressed. He either went out and bought himself another rare book—or asked Rosenbach, the first-editions dealers, to buy one for him—or sat himself down at the piano and wrote something that would do better.

Betty Kern was now getting an education in the widest sense of the term. She crossed the Atlantic on the Olympic with her parents, and vacationed with them at Palm Beach. Her schooling was fitted in somewhere in between, and all the time she recalls 'waking up and going to sleep to the sound of music'. Her nurse, who 'adored Jerry', still watched over her every moment until she was 12, and school was still a misery for her. She felt a misfit, dreading the comments that would be made when her schoolmates saw the nurse accompanying her to and from school. But at home or on holiday, life was practically idyllic. Her father doted on her; he was interested in everything; his maxim was that life was to be enjoyed, and the very notion of boredom was something he was not prepared to countenance. He bought Betty board games, and if these were not to her taste he invented new ones, and helped her do jigsaws and crossword puzzles.

Betty was eight years old when Jerry had his next huge success. His show *Sunny*—a single-word title that was immediately reminiscent of *Sally* and was forever after to be confused with its predecessor—once more starred Marilyn Miller. This time, however, the show was presented by Charles Dillingham and not by her paramour, Ziegfeld. It also had as its standard, a song with a one-word title that deserves more than a mere mention in the Kern story. 'Who' is Kern at his very best, with the one word held on a single note lasting perhaps longer than any other in popular song.

Even more important, the show marked the beginning of a collaboration which, if Jerry had wanted it, might have become one of the great permanent partnerships of show business. It was the professional introduction of Kern to Oscar Hammerstein II, then the 30-year-old son of the theatre manager William Hammerstein and grandson of the first Oscar Hammerstein, whose Victoria Theatre was one of the great temples of vaudeville. They had first met the year before at the funeral of Victor Herbert. (No one now talked of Kern's taking on Herbert's mantle; indeed, rather that Herbert had been something of a Kern of his day.) The first day they got together to discuss *Sunny*, Jerry did not go near the piano. He had to see the libretto before he was prepared to even consider a score. When he conceded it had some merit, the two planned the songs they would produce.

Hammerstein was not Jerry's only collaborator on the show. He shared the credits for book and lyrics with the German-born Otto Harbach. Both men were as nervous and apprehensive as was any new Kern lyricist. Would the great man throw his weight around? Would he treat their work disdainfully? Would he, in short, be hard to get along with? Certainly there was never any question in their minds as to who was boss. Jerome Kern could never have been party to an arrangement like that of Rodgers and Hammerstein. He regarded the music in a song as far more important than the words; yet even so, he demanded that the verses presented to him should never do less than enhance his own creation.

Hammerstein wrote that Kern's impatience with incompetence was nothing compared with his intolerance of incompetent people who masqueraded as geniuses. What he found difficult to understand at first was Kern's attitude to his own work. When he called on Jerry, expecting him to be bustling with energy and determination, he found him instead deeply involved with a new puzzle which could not possibly be interrupted by a mere piece of composition. And if Jerry wanted to work at a dawdling pace, no amount of enthusiasm on anyone else's part could persuade him to hurry. However, if Jerry didn't keep office hours, he was a disciplined songwriter; he was not one of those who waited for a panicky telephone call before he began work, or until the deadline approached menacingly. He knew what he wanted to write and he got on with writing it. The fact that it was a Saturday, a Sunday or Thanksgiving did not make the slightest difference to him. 'I don't let a single day pass without writing something,' he said once, as though that day just had to be recorded in some way, as another man might write a diary. And he was still as excited about his work as when he had first heard people humming 'They Didn't Believe Me'. When something pleased him, he reacted in short, sporadic bursts: 'Marvellous', 'Wonderful', 'Couldn't be better'.

By this time—no doubt much to Eva's relief—he had become an inveterate user of the telephone. He frequently answered it himself now—taking down detailed messages from the butcher or grocer in printed capitals. He always found it easier to read his own notes when written that way and most of his friends agreed.

His memos about *Sunny* were similarly documented. They mostly reiterated his hatred of the fragmented use of speciality acts without any particular reference to the sequence of the plot. Ukelele Ike (Cliff Edwards), for instance, had to appear on stage in the course of the evening strumming his ukelele. Writing this into the plot was made even more difficult by the fact that Edwards's contract specified he had to do his 'thing' between 10 and 10.15 p.m. The story, therefore, had to be framed around that bizarre stipulation. In addition, Jack Donaghue, Ziegfeld's great rival for Marilyn Miller's affections, was expected to dance, and so were the other stars, Clifton Webb and Mary Hay. It would all have made a much better

Ziegfeld Follies than a 'legitimate' show.

For nearly an hour, Dillingham and his writers went through the story line with Marilyn Miller in Dillingham's book-lined, wood-panelled office. Every complete number was gone over, with Jerry inserting his own instructions. Finally, Miss Miller called out in her little high-pitched voice: 'When do I do my tap speciality?'

It has been suggested that Jerry's song numbers with Harbach sound as if they had been created in the tradition of German operetta rather than that of Broadway. Since Kern always wrote the music first, it is difficult to understand why this should be. However, Harbach was to say of his first collaboration with Jerry: 'If something was the least bit out of balance I had to iron it out, for he was a purist. However, if I brought in a lyric that really hit him, after working it over, he would give the piano keys a bang then get up and throw his arms around me.' It was Jerry's favourite way of showing his enthusiasm. 'He always looked for the gimmick to make a song logical within the play and was delighted when a song had good motivation,' he said years later.

Right from the beginning, there was no doubt that the motivation of *Sunny* was right. The fact that 'Who' and the title song, 'Sunny', were the first two numbers in the show gives some idea of the degree of investment of his talent that Kern had put into the production. They were the best, but the songs that followed were good enough to keep the audience's feet tapping for the next two and a half hours or so, too. The story concerned a bare-back rider in a circus who marries the wrong man—and is always conscious that the right one will be waiting for her. The songs sounded better than the dramatic action; fortunately, the costumes and sets were better, too, and one of the special effects was a real circus tent which blew about in a realistic wind.

Sunny was as well received as *Sally* had been and ran for almost as long—517 performances at the New Amsterdam Theatre, followed by a number of road companies. When the show hit London, the critics were ecstatic. It starred Binnie Hale in the Marilyn Miller part, and Jack Buchanan, who was to be known as Britain's answer to Fred Astaire—and at that time was doing even better as a 'single': Fred was still part of a duo with his sister Adele. But it was Kern's music that got the loudest plaudits. The *Daily Express* reported: 'When, to a chorus of "Who Stole My Heart Away? Who?", the curtain fell at the end of *Sunny* last night, the Hippodrome had obviously a success equal to *Mercenary Mary*.' (There could be no higher praise, since *Mercenary Mary* had been a box office blockbuster for months.) 'There are no fewer than 15 scenes, which begin in the circus and finish in Florida. There is a circus parade, including a dwarf, a giant, a snake charmer and a fat lady; a wedding on board ship and a poppy field. There is scarcely any jazz. In fact it is all charming.'

Scarcely any jazz. No wonder Jerry was pleased with the way the show was staged. But he could still be difficult. In 1926, he joined the Dramatists Guild, which established a closed shop; outside it no one could ever get a play or the songs for a show performed on the Broadway stage. He was in company with Guy Bolton, Noël Coward, George Gershwin, James Gleason, Somerset Maugham, Eugene O'Neill and about 120 or so others, whose aim was to fight what then appeared the threat of the Hollywood studios to the New York theatre.

Jerry was not overly preoccupied with the problem. Practically nothing could stop his work from being performed anywhere that he wanted. He was more concerned, it seemed, with such minor irritations as the pretentions of show girls. One young lady in particular affected what she believed to be the enticing mannerism of rolling her 'r's. Jerry found it unbearable.

'Tell me, Mr. Kern,' she said, fluttering her long eyelashes to the point where they almost caused a draught, 'tell me—you want me to c-rr-ross the stage, but I'm behind a table. How shall I get ac-r-r-oss?'

Jerry could not resist. 'How do you get across?' he asked. 'Why, my dear, just r-r-roll over on your 'r's.'

Because Jerry set competitive standards for other people, a constant effort was made by some of his acquaintances to show that they were every bit as good as he considered himself to be. Once, a chorus girl carefully arranged to have herself dropped outside the theatre in a huge limousine—because she had seen Jerry waiting at the stage-door.

Kern realized what she was trying to do. As she alighted

from the car, carefully lifting her skirt to show a pair of well-shaped silk-covered calves, Jerry could not resist commenting, 'It just shows you what some girls will do to get noticed.'

The dancer was stung. 'Just for that,' she retorted, 'I'll arrive next time in a Rolls Royce.'

'No . . .' replied Kern, 'not just for *that*, you won't.'

Meanwhile, he had plans for more new shows. They would not all be like *Sunny*. *The City Chap*, based on Winchell Smith's play *The Fortune Hunter* and also presented by Dillingham, was another partnership with Anne Caldwell. But none of the songs —'Like The Nymphs Of Spring', 'Saratoga', 'No One Knows' —were classic Kern, and the show limped off the Liberty Theatre stage after a mere 72 performances.

Criss Cross, his only Broadway show in 1926, did somewhat better. Again it was presented by Dillingham and again there were lyrics and book by Anne Caldwell, assisted this time by Otto Harbach. Audiences heard 'Hydrophobia Blues', 'Cinderella Girl', 'I Love My Little Susie' and 'Kiss A Four Leaf Clover' all of 206 times.

Jerry collaborated with Harbach again at the beginning of 1927 on *Lucky*. It lacked a single memorable tune; not even the New Amsterdam Theatre could make *Lucky* live up to its name. It lasted for just 71 performances.

Far from being depressed by this flop, Jerry was concentrating on the future. He had been doing a great deal of reading. And one book in particular had captured his imagination.

Show Boat

DEFINING GENIUS IS difficult. Yet it can be simply the ability to take advantage of a series of lucky breaks and out of them create something the world cannot thereafter imagine being without.

It was coincidence that led Edna Ferber to write *Show Boat* and luck that made Jerome Kern think about turning it into a Broadway spectacular. It was his genius that created in 'Ol' Man River' not just a hit tune but a folksong so convincing that many believed—and still do believe—it to be a traditional Negro melody. A generation later Mrs. Oscar Hammerstein was to say 'It was my husband who wrote "Ol' Man River", Jerry Kern wrote "Dum-di-dah-dah, di-dum-di-dah-dah . . ."' That, perhaps, was more than just a matter of semantics. It *was* a magnificent collaboration, but it cannot be denied that the majesty of 'Ol' Man River' was essentially the result of Kern's insight into traditional Negro music which never allowed him to stoop to parody. Hammerstein would probably never have been able to write such wonderful lyrics to a less worthy tune.

And neither of them would have written *Show Boat* had not Edna Ferber first produced her book—and she maintained that she would never have written it had she not taken a lazy stroll in Washington Park, Chicago, one day in 1921. She overheard three old men, residents of a nearby home for the aged, solving

85

the problems of the world as they sat on a park bench. It gave her the idea for a short story which she called *Old Man Minick* and which in turn became a play that she co-wrote with the eminent dramatist George Kaufman.

The play was produced in an old disused theatre in New London, Connecticut, which had been out of action for so long that on the first night there were as many bats in the balcony as there were paying customers. At the end of the evening's performance, the wealthy 'angel' who had financed the production said that next time, perhaps it would be more sensible to do the try-out on a show boat.

'A what?' asked Miss Ferber.

'A showboat,' replied Mr. Winthrup Ames, the wealthy benefactor.

'What's a show boat?'

Mr. Ames explained that for 60 years or more river boats had been chugging down the Mississippi producing melodramas and comedies for the benefit of passengers.

Miss Ferber, who had a keen eye for observation and a reputation for being able to capture real life in her writing, was amazed that the show boats, such a marvellously colourful source for a story, were virtually unchronicled. Like an intrepid hunter in search of a rare specimen of wild life, she set about looking for a show boat. She found one in North Carolina, called the Pamlico River, on which the James Adams Floating Palace Theatre nightly regaled the assembled crowds with its latest dramatic exhibition. She ate with the company, sat in the box office, and watched the players march in red-coated finery through the streets of the show boat's ports of call, drumming up business like a circus parade. And, having now won the Pulitzer Prize for her book *So Big*, Miss Ferber used her experiences to write the novel *Show Boat* about the good ship Cotton Blossom. It was also the tale of Gaylord Ravenal (never did a name more aptly convey the character of a man), the river gambler, his girl Magnolia, and Julie, the show boat singer forced to leave the boat when she admits to having Negro blood in her veins.

The book was an almost instant success. Jerry Kern, who liked to keep up with the contemporary literary scene as much as he loved studying a treasured antique volume, read the

With Jean Harlow on the set of Reckless.　　　(Kobal Collection)

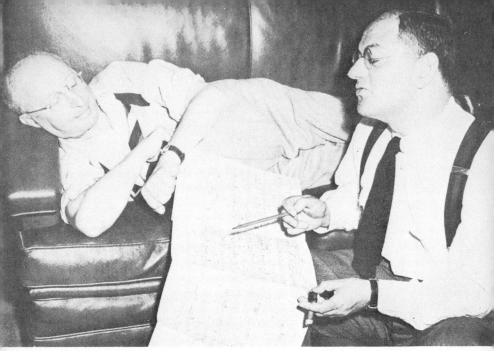

Kern working with Ira Gershwin on Cover Girl. (Courtesy Ira Gershwi

Robert Walker as Jerry and Dorothy Patrick as Eva in Till the Clouds Roll By. *The scene illustrates their first meeting at Walton-on-Thames.*

(Kobal Collectio

In his library with grandson Steven, 1943.

Kern with Betty, 1944.

Probably the last photograph of Kern, with Betty, Steven and Eva, 1945.

opening chapters of *Show Boat* and took a step that was rare for a composer: he bought the theatrical rights. Then he arranged for Alexander Woolcott to introduce him to the writer when she attended the opening of *Criss Cross*. They were so impressed with each other that there was no doubt they would get along. Next Kern rang Oscar Hammerstein with just one question: 'How would you like to do a show for Ziegfeld? It's got a million-dollar title, *Show Boat*. Get a copy and read it right away.'

Hammerstein had a question of his own: 'Is Ziegfeld enthusiastic?'

Jerry was his usual straightforward self: 'He doesn't know anything about it yet.'

It did not take long for Ziegfeld to get to know about *Show Boat*. Kern bombarded him with the idea at a series of meetings, in phone calls and over dinner parties. Finally, the showman succumbed. He was opening a new theatre—called appropriately, the Ziegfeld—and *Show Boat*, he conceded, might be ideal for the grand opening. However, as the months went by, he put off the decision. 'Not quite ready yet,' he stuttered every time Kern and Hammerstein raised the issue. The truth was that Ziegfeld was running out of money. Both composer and lyricist eventually agreed that the time had come to stop prevaricating. They called at Ziegfeld's luxurious home and were shown into the bathroom, where Flo was being shaved by his own personal barber. After sharing Ziegfeld's 'snack'— roast beef and champagne—they left. Neither of them had had the courage to confront him about the decision.

In the meantime, both Kern and Hammerstein set about soaking up the atmosphere of the show boats. They talked endlessly about the characters of the book and how each could be translated to the stage. As Hammerstein said later: 'We had fallen hopelessly in love with it. We couldn't keep our hands off it. We had ourselves swooning.' They practically retraced Edna Ferber's steps up the gangplank of the Pamlico River. They sought out every show boat they could find, watched the shows, studied the people coming aboard, and gambled with them at the card tables. On the banks of the river, they watched bales of cotton being handled by men whose fathers, grandfathers and great-grandfathers had done the same soul-destroying and back-breaking work, singing as they laboured.

As he watched and listened, Jerry recalled a Black singer whom he had heard at a New York concert a few weeks before. He couldn't remember the man's name but the deep bass voice remained with him. Now the memory of that voice combined with those he had heard on the river bank. The memory became even more acute when Jerry read Mark Twain's *Life On The Mississippi*. With every word, Kern not only felt the wash of the river against the show boat's paddles, but could virtually smell the flotsam in the water—and always there was that deep anonymous voice throbbing at the back of his mind. The rhythms stayed with him all the way back home, where the first thing he did was to go to the piano and tap out the one particular melody that had haunted him all the time. It was the 'dum-di-dah-dah, di-dum-di-dah-dah' that became 'Ol' Man River'. He finished it in five minutes. By the time Ham—merstein took over, the song conveyed all the sympathy and understanding that both instantly felt for a people who then seemed to be forever condemned to a life not far from slavery.

Jerry had no idea that he was in any way producing an historic document. He just wanted his songs to sound right. And he just as easily scribbled and then fully annotated his songs on the back of some other manuscript or on the blank side of a private letter, as on a virgin pad. Today, the only extant Kern manuscript is one that he wrote 13 years after *Show Boat*.

Anyone eavesdropping on the pair of collaborators as they worked on *Show Boat* might have been forgiven for thinking that the rest of the score tumbled off Jerry's piano and bounced onto Oscar Hammerstein's notebook with an almost casual ease. But after the inspiration came the hard work. Usually, they did not work together in the same room. Frequently, Oscar would phone Jerry and sing him the lyrics he had prepared for a tune. Occasionally they argued, but disagreements were rare. It was obvious very early on that their ideas made them entirely compatible.

However, though the work progressed well, at one stage it looked as though there might be no Broadway opening. It was not an easy decision to make when he had men of the calibre of Kern and Hammerstein working for him, but Ziegfeld was less and less convinced that *Show Boat* was strong enough to be the opening production at his new theatre. Finally, he gave instructions for the much more traditional *Rio Rita* to be the opening engagement.

When it opened on February 2, 1927, Ziegfeld promised Kern and Hammerstein that *Show Boat* would get its première after *Rio Rita*. But *Rio Rita* did better than anyone anticipated, and it was not until December, after 494 performances, that the show reached the end of the road. At last *Show Boat* was ready for its spectacular Broadway opening.

Because it was a Ziegfeld show, no detail had been over-looked. The river and the river boat settings had to be almost indistinguishable from the real thing. However, because no one wanted to discard any part of what was clearly a production in which most of the aces had come up trumps, the show over-ran. It began at 8.15 on the night of its Washington try-out and lasted until 30 minutes past midnight. Plainly it had to be cut. Unfortunately, Jerry felt that the spirited Helen Morgan who was playing the night club singer, Julie, had such an exciting voice that she needed at least one other song to exploit it. For a scene in which Julie, now on dry land, rehearsed her act, Jerry felt he had just the right tune—that is, if Oscar Hammer-stein had no objections. For the song he had in mind was not one of Oscar's but 'Bill', rejected from two previous productions but now, he was sure, perfect for the setting.

When Helen was first handed the number, she sang it perched on top of the piano. 'That's it,' cried Jerry, as usual proving to be as much unpaid producer as composer. 'That's how you have to sing it.' Hammerstein had no objection to the number being included. Neither did Ziegfeld—providing the time could be found. But that was not the end of the matter. Quite clearly, Wodehouse would have to give his agreement. He did as soon as he was asked, but there was still another hurdle to be overcome. Guy Bolton had rights in it, too—because he and Wodehouse were still splitting their royalties.

'You can't do it unless you pay me my share,' said Bolton. He and Hammerstein met and there were some tough words. Eventually, the two of them drew up a contract, promising Bolton an appropriate share in the royalties. (Bolton is appar-ently still smarting at the fact that when *Show Boat* was revived in London in 1971, half of the royalties for 'Bill' went to the Hammerstein estate—and he has still not been able to get his hands on the cash. According to Bolton, 'Bill' remained a sore point with Hammerstein who never liked the idea of *Show Boat* having a song with anyone else's lyrics but his own. When the 1935 film was made, Hammerstein changed some of 'Bill's' words—in order, Bolton alleged, that he could claim authorship of the song. Bolton says that neither he nor Wodehouse ever got any income from the film's royalties.)

It was during the show's Washington try-out that Kern and Hammerstein decided there was a song in it that neither of them liked very much, and agreed that a substitute had to be prepared. Jerry gave Oscar a couple of sheets of music and the next day Hammerstein had a lyric to go with it. As Kern read the words, his short grey hair bristled, his eyes protruded, and if he could have adjusted the angle of his head, he would have done so. Right from the earliest days of their collaboration, Jerry had told Oscar: 'Don't write anything with the word "cupid" in it. I can't stand cupids.' But here was a song called 'Cupid Knows The Way', with Cupid featuring in practically every line. Finally, Jerry caught the glint in Oscar's eye. He had been the victim of a leg-pull that at one stage had looked as though it might be the cause of an acute case of cardiac arrest. When Jerry was handed the real words, his relief was so great that he threw his arms around Oscar's neck. 'Cupid' had become 'Why Do I Love You'. Generations of admirers would prove equally grateful. As the show went from one try-out date to the next, Kern and Hammerstein grew closer. They ate together, they laughed together, and Oscar's young son, William, got to know Jerry so well that the composer became an uncle-figure to him.

At Philadelphia, Jerry noticed that wherever Hammerstein went a young woman was lurking in the background. 'Who,' he asked, 'is that "Mona Lisa" over there?' The nickname endeared him forever to the girl Hammerstein later introduced as Dorothy, who was soon to become the second Mrs. Oscar Hammerstein.

The Black chorus paid Jerry an unexpected compliment: one after another, the singers and dancers told him that they could not understand how a white man could possibly produce music like that of 'Ol' Man River'. Several were sure they'd heard the song when they were children. They hadn't. There is not a tune in Black folk music that even resembles 'Ol' Man River', but it could so easily have been plucked from folk memory. 'You make it sound that way,' Jerry told one singer generously. 'Characters write their own music.'

Right from the beginning, Kern had wanted the young Negro bass who had inspired 'Ol' Man River' to be the one to sing it in the show. But the man could not be traced until after Jules Bledscoe had been signed and had triumphed on the opening night. The elusive bass? A certain Paul Robeson.

The partnership between Kern and Edna Ferber was a harmonious one all the way along—partly, perhaps, because they shared the same financial adviser, William Kron, but mainly because each had a profound respect for the work of the other. Just as Jerry had never had any pretensions to writing good lyrics, so he recognized the importance of a good story by a gifted writer. And Edna was flattered by his enthusiasm for *Show Boat*, not only as theatre entertainment, but as the vehicle through which an American audience would first accept what one critic described as 'literate and sophisticated musical drama'.

When *Show Boat* finally anchored at the Ziegfeld on December 27, 1927, there was no need to think of bringing in any other talent. A cast that in addition to Bledscoe and Helen Morgan featured Charles Winninger as Captain Andy, Edna May Oliver as Queenie and Howard Marsh as Gaylord Ravenal was enough to satisfy not just Mr. Ziegfeld and his two writers but the audience and the critics. From the first curtain, it was clear that *Show Boat* was the realization of Kern's dream of a big Broadway show with a big Broadway story. *Rose Marie* and *New Moon* had both had drama in them before *Show Boat*, but there had never been a musical with as fully-constructed a plot as this, in which the songs were as important to the story line as the dialogue.

George Jean Nathan was to say about *Show Boat*: 'In the first place, you really believe in its love story. In most musicals, even in some of the better ones, if the music didn't distract you and hypnotize you into suspending judgement, you wouldn't believe for a moment that any such ass as the hero could conceivably arouse tender passions in the heroine or that even any such spongecake as the latter could operate likewise in the case of the aforesaid half-wit. The story of Magnolia and Gaylord Ravenal does, however, somehow succeed in pleasing you that you forgot to bring along a tomato. It has gentleness and tenderness and charm, and over it hovers the scent of years that were fragrant. In the second place, there is inherent in the book a colour seldom found in most shows. In these others the missing colour is hopefully relegated to the costumes, scenery and lighting effects. In *Show Boat* it emanates not only from the dialogue, but from the music . . . It confidently invites response without resort to those vaudeville speciality acts, arty ballets and other irrelevancies which are included in most musical exhibits. It recognizes its beginning, middle and end and it sticks more or less resolutely to them.'

The New York Times described it as 'just about the best musical piece ever to arrive' under Ziegfeld's patronage. It had, said the paper, 'about every ingredient that the perfect song and dance concoction should have . . . In its adherence to the story, it is positively slavish. The adaptation of the novel has been intelligently made and such liberties as the demands of musical comedy do not twist the tale nor distort its values. For this and for the far better-than-average lyrics with which it is endowed credit Oscar Hammerstein II who is rapidly monopolizing the function of author for the town's musical entertainments. Then, too, *Show Boat* has an exceptionally tuneful score, the most lilting and satisfactory that the wily Jerome Kern has contrived in several seasons. Potential song hits were as common last night as top hats. *Show Boat* is an excellent musical comedy, one that comes perilously close to being the best the town has seen in several seasons.'

The potential hits became actual ones, as every single history of the American theatre will confirm—not just 'Ol' Man River', 'Bill' and 'Why Do I Love You', but 'Only Make Believe', a classic of its kind, 'Can't Help Lovin' Dat Man', and a nice piece of theatricality called 'Life Upon The Wicked Stage' which, while never approaching the popularity of the others, finds a place in every Kern anthology. It is Jerry at his most sardonically funny.

Eva loved the show. Her arms went round her husband's

neck that first night and the real love she felt for him was never more publicly expressed. She always said thereafter that it was a tune from *Show Boat* that was her favourite—not one of the most popular standards, but one whose sentiment she took for herself, 'You Are Love'. As for Jerry, like many another song-writer who must always be part businessman, his favourite was the one that became the biggest hit. 'Ol' Man River', of course. From the moment that he returned home to Bronxville after *Show Boat*'s first night, he would play 'Ol' Man River' every time he left for a trip and whenever he returned. It became his good luck talisman.

The show itself was brimful of good luck. It ran for two years at the Ziegfeld and took in something like $50,000 a week. When it moved to London the following March, Kern had replaced the singer of 'Ol' Man River' with a man who had unexpectedly caused a sensation in what was supposed to be the completely straight play, *Emperor Jones*. He had used his deep bass to chant a spiritual, and the director was so overcome that he had asked him to sing much more. It was, of course, Paul Robeson. Robeson was the undoubted hit of the London *Show Boat* opening, even though he had only one song to sing and the listed stars were Edith Day and Marie Burke. He recorded 'Ol' Man River' with the Drury Lane Orchestra, but a contractual agreement (that the only recordings from the show that would be allowed were those by the New York cast) meant that his disc was never released. It is now a collector's item.

Just before the first night curtain went up at Drury Lane, a letter was received by the President of the Gallery First Nighters —a club made up of serious theatregoers who never missed an opening and who always saw the show from the highest and cheapest balcony. It protested at the employment of coloured American artists in London while an embargo had been placed on the employment of English actors and actresses in New York.

The show, nevertheless, had a rapturous welcome. Hannen Swaffer wrote in the *Daily Express*: 'The show wants only more humour—and more of Paul Robeson.'

Soon after the London opening, the show transferred—with French translation—to Paris. In 1929 it was filmed with

Joseph Schildkraut and Alma Rubens and with a score which included not only a lot of Stephen Foster but which was also originally planned to have a wholly different set of songs. Billy Rose, an entrepreneur impresario with lyric-writing aspirations, heard that Carl Laemmle Junior, son of the very successful film producer, was being put in charge of making the movie version of the show. He button-holed Laemmle and told him that he simply had to throw out 'the terrible original score'. New songs were written, but fortunately for *Show Boat* and for the good health of Mr. Laemmle and Mr. Rose, once Jerome Kern got to hear about it, the idea of a new score was abandoned.

Other films of *Show Boat*, however, did follow, with a slight change in characterization and with musical alterations, too. The 1935 film version (with Charles Winninger and the additional advantages of Irene Dunne and Allan Jones) starred Paul Robeson and featured a new song, 'I Still Suits Me'— obviously as a vehicle for Robeson to do more than 'Ol' Man River', which was all the stage show ever allowed him to do. In 1951, when *Show Boat* was filmed again, the song was dropped. Ava Gardner as the mixed-blooded Julie looked even less dark-skinned than she had as an Anglo-Indian in *Bowani Junction*, and William Warfield in the Robeson role was practically the only representative of the Black race in the whole picture. Howard Keel, as Gaylord, also miraculously failed to age much beyond 40, instead of being at least 60 as the character had been in all the other versions.

In 1932, *Show Boat* went back to Broadway—this time at the Casino Theatre and with Robeson for the first time showing American audiences how superbly he and 'Ol' Man River' went together. So superbly, in fact, that no other version ever sounds quite right.

Fourteen years later, *Show Boat* was once more at her home port, the Ziegfeld Theatre on Sixth Avenue. Not a revival, Hammerstein said at the time, 'because that sounds like warmed-over theatrical fare'. It was, he declared, a new production and well received it was, too. Lewis Nichols wrote in *The New York Times*: ' "Ol' Man River" still rolls along and *Show Boat* still is one of the real musicals of the modern American stage. As it returned . . . its music was unstaled by repetition, its familiar lyrics seemed new.' In another piece, he said: 'An opening night audience in New York has the reputation of being hard to live with, of sitting with a sneer and daring the performers to offer entertainment. This was not true for that at *Show Boat*. Instead, it dared the performers not to be good. Had Kenneth Spencer failed to do rightly by "Ol' Man River" the first four rows of the orchestra would have climbed onto the stage and handed him to the side of the Cotton Blossom. Mr. Spencer is alive today.'

The New York Times had a love affair with the 'revival', for despite Mr. Hammerstein, that was precisely what it was. Ward Monkhouse wrote: 'Here's a musical play with beauty, pathos, nostalgia, panoramic pattern and a Jerome Kern score that will endure for as long as the theatre exists. If in this 1946 version of the Kern-Hammerstein-Ferber classic, the story now runs down and runs somewhat to patness in its final phases, if portions of the narrative now seem a bit laboured and if a few of the present players are not up to the form of their predecessors, these faults are but minor. The Kern music is still overpoweringly beautiful. The production is stunning. Jan Clayton is a fragile and lovely Magnolia and Carole Bruce, in a role forever to be associated with the melancholy and legendary Helen Morgan, comes through wonderfully. Saturday evening was Kern's as it should have been and as Oscar Hammerstein wanted it to be . . . *Show Boat*, a timeless memorial to the genius of Jerome Kern, is now, 19 years after its original production, the best buy in the theatre of New York. The town is in the debt of Oscar Hammerstein for bringing it back.'

Show Boat has survived mainly because there was a timelessness about the story, set though it was in such a colourful era. The music, brought up to date with arrangements more suited to the era in which they are played, has transferred equally well from one age to another. The lyrics have needed changing hardly at all. That is not entirely the case with the dialogue. Oscar Hammerstein could not have been expected to appreciate that sentences like 'Gay looks a bit queer today' might have a totally different meaning nearly half a century later.

The films have not always come off as well as the shows. In 1951, Otis L. Guernsey Jr. wrote in the *New York Herald Tribune* of the last of the productions: 'This *Show Boat* is so

95

much a summer-styled presentation that it is directed by George Sidney in a hurry to get over the incidents in the story and set the extras to whirling in production numbers. The memorable scene in which Julie's husband borrows blood from her arm in order to claim to the sheriff that technically he has Negro blood in him is tossed off here in nearly ludicrous fashion. Characteristically, this instance of real drama is minimized but its sentimental aftermath, the expulsion of the couple from the show boat and from town is dwelt upon lovingly. It is as though the intent was to keep *Show Boat* devoid of real feeling in order to preserve the empty decorum of a lightweight and soft-hearted musical panorama.' As for Ava Gardner's performance, the critic was equally merciless: 'She handles "Bill" and "Can't Help Lovin' Dat Man" as though she were posing for a series of risqué photographs, but the songs retain a charm that rises above the treatment.'

In the 1960s, the show once more opened all over the United States—with the addition of 'I Still Suits Me'—and in 1971 it opened for its long run at London's Adelphi Theatre. Like the river, there was never any reason to suppose that *Show Boat* would not just keep rollin' along.

Don't Tempt Me

IT MIGHT BE THOUGHT that after the success of *Show Boat*, Kern would decide it should set the pattern for all his future work. Instead, he continued much as before, hoping always that the songs fitted well into the plot and that every time he had a big hit on his hands. He knew it was far from likely. Composing, he said, was 'like fishing. You get a nibble, but you don't know whether it's a minnow or a marlin until you reel it in. You write 20 tunes to get two good ones—and the wastebasket yearns for music.'

He was working once more in England, admitting to Eva and friends that he enjoyed being in London as much as anything else because it gave him such a wonderful opportunity to visit the second-hand book shops of Charing Cross Road. But the shows he wrote were all specifically for the British market.

Blue Eyes, which he and Guy Bolton wrote for the opening of the Piccadilly Theatre, was a story based on the Bonnie Prince Charlie legend. No one expected it to be transferred to Broadway, and rightly so. It was no *Show Boat*. As *The Times* remarked: 'Alas that the tale is meant to be taken so seriously! It is quite prettily contrived and adorned here and there by shrewd, laughing musical comedy . . . there are no concerted dances, no feasts of smiling enthusiasm or athletic precision . . . Even the sentimental songs are weighted by the general

97

solemnity . . . Mr. Jerome Kern's music is neither very striking nor very obtrusive. No doubt it serves its purpose very well.'

At least Jerry had the satisfaction of having written a song called 'The Banks of Loch Lomond' and hearing it splendidly sung by a male chorus.

The programme at the Piccadilly established Jerry's credentials, no doubt to his satisfaction: 'Mr. Jerome Kern, the composer of *Blue Eyes*, is so well known to music-loving audiences both sides of the Atlantic, that they scarcely need to be reminded of his musical contributions to international gaiety and an abbreviated list of his successes is sufficient to substantiate the fact that it is to Mr. Kern we owe the present harmonic treatment of light music which finds such favourable acceptance both in London and New York.'

The show lasted for 276 performances—including the period when it transferred to Daly's Theatre so that the Piccadilly could be converted temporarily into a cinema to show Al Jolson's *The Singing Fool*, the first talkie seen in London.

Back home again, Jerry and Eva continued to shower their love and affection on little Betty. They bought her a horse— which was the beginning of a lifelong love affair with the animals (she breeds them today at her home in Kentucky), although when it became obvious that the family were travelling around too much to be able to devote to it the personal attention it needed, the horse was sold. Betty loved horse shows, but Jerry would not allow her to show horses herself. It was about the only time he refused his daughter anything.

Jerry was now 43, certain that he had had his share of good fortune. Once, he and Eva talked about the future and about the inevitability of death. 'When you have to go,' he told her fatalistically, 'you have to go.' Eva on the other hand was a great clinger to life and refused to contemplate death as even a remote possibility. As far as she was concerned, she was as immortal as Jerry's music, or his library.

He would spend hours shut away with a book and when he was not actually reading or lovingly fingering a volume, it seemed he was searching for another one. And then quite suddenly he came to the one conclusion that anyone knowing him would have considered to be the very last to enter his thoughts. 'The books are possessing me, instead of my possessing them,' he said. 'I'm going to sell the lot.'

It took Jerry just 15 minutes to make up his mind to put his library under the auctioneer's hammer. Without any warning to Eva he decided: 'The library is beyond my mode of life.' He revealed for the first time that the books were his only reason for keeping a full staff on at the house at Bronxville. They were never kept under lock and key, never in strong-boxes. He enjoyed surrounding himself with them. 'They were like friends whom I wanted always about me,' he said. In fact, his passion for them was much deeper. He could no longer trust himself to give them the care they deserved without every other thing in his life suffering.

What made him give way to his sudden impulse was the realization of their value. What if one were to get slightly damaged? It was a chilling thought. When a dealer friend told him that on his mantelpiece he had a collection of first editions of Dickens which alone were worth $30,000, he felt he had to do something. He not only had every Dickens first edition, but also Dickens memorabilia—including the novelist's marriage licence and a letter from him to a Professor Felton of New York, giving the news of his impending divorce from Catherine: 'We have tried all other things and they have all broken down under us.' He had three pages of the manuscript of *Oliver Twist* and Dickens's own notebook—28 pages crammed full of plots, dialogues, names of characters, written between 1855 and the end of his life.

Jerry owned an uncut first edition of *Pride and Prejudice*; a first edition of *Jane Eyre*. He had the complete signed manuscript of Byron's *Marino Faliero, Doge of Venice*. There was also a first edition of *Alice in Wonderland*, and one of *Robinson Crusoe*, and another of *Gulliver's Travels*. And he had Shelley's own copy of his *Queen Mab*. He collected books connected with Robert and Elizabeth Browning, and had not only an original edition of Elizabeth Barrett's first work—published by her father when she was still a young girl—but a copy of Robert Browning's *Pauline*, a first edition in its original covers.

His first purchase had cost him $40; his most recent acquisition had cost exactly 1,000 times that. But he was excluding both his first and last buys from the sale. It wasn't just a question of economics. 'I never thought much about monetary value when buying books,' he explained as arrangements were made for the sale at New York's Anderson Galleries. 'I set out to collect a library of distinguished volumes of association and sentimental interest.' He would never reveal the titles of either the first or the last book he had bought. He also made sure that none of the books that had been presented to him as gifts were included in the sale. That would have offended his sense of propriety.

On January 1, 1929, an intrigued crowd of bibliophiles thronged the Anderson Galleries for the opening of the sale. When the sale catalogue was first issued, it became clear that it was going to be one of the biggest book sales of the century. One of the first books to go under the hammer was Robert Burns's *Poems Chiefly in the Scottish Dialect*. The book—it was not even a first edition, but a second printing—went for $23,500. It was a good augury for the rest of the 1,500 lots. The evening ended with just 153 books sold—bringing in a staggering $166,363. At that rate, conjectured *The New York Times*, the whole library would be worth more than $1 million. The rare edition of Browning's *Pauline* went for $16,000. The uncut *Pride and Prejudice*, however, earned a mere $4,800.

Jerry revelled in the attention being given to his possessions. It was not like other sales when famous men have been forced to part with treasured belongings out of dire financial necessity. Jerry was selling simply because he had decided to do so, and consequently was enjoying it immensely. He was witnessing it all with feelings of relief, he said: 'As my collection has grown, books have not only fascinated me; they have enslaved me. As rare books became rarer, I battled for them, treasured them and so became a collector. I never captured a prize. The prize always encaptured me.'

On the second evening, there were even more people crowding into the galleries—men in tuxedoes, women in long dresses, who quite obviously regarded it as a prelude to the evening's entertainment. Jerry managed to view the entire proceedings with an air of detached excitement that he could never muster for the more usual evening performances in which he was involved. That night, $615,387 was raised. 'It's a bull market,' roared one satisfied customer who had decided to put his money into books when every other rich man seemed to be going into stocks and shares. He could have had no idea how clever he was. When he bought the first edition of *Pickwick Papers* for $28,000, he was establishing a world record high— only nine years earlier Jerry had bought it for $3,500. Altogether, the Dickens collection went for $273,952.

By January 10, the progress of the sale was being followed by newspaper readers with the avidity usually reserved for a serial yarn. A first edition of Fielding's *The History of Tom Jones* fetched $29,000, and the news was published all over the world. In Britain, the events at the gallery filled column after column in the newspapers, under the simple heading: 'The Kern Sale'.

At the end of the fifth day a total of $933,625 had come in with still half the lots as yet unsold. On January 21, the sixth day of the auction, a Charles Lamb manuscript realized $48,000, part of $221,490 worth of sales that night. In many cases, books were fetching 100 times their 1914 value.

The London *Daily Mail* used the sale as a convenient excuse for America-baiting: 'A potent reason for these abnormal prices is the American collectors' lack of originality. They all want the same books. Hardy and Dickens are the fashion. Tennyson and Swinburne are out of favour.' But there were many notable buyers at the sale who plainly did know what they were doing. The celebrated Dr. Rosenbach was locked in competition with another dealer for a succession of books, and for quite a time this duel provided at least half the fun of the proceedings.

The sale also gave Kern his revenge on the dealer who many years earlier had engaged him in conversation while an assistant slyly changed the price tag from $2,000 to $6,500 on a Robert Burns inscribed first edition. The same dealer now bought his book back for $23,000.

Finally, much to the relief of a lot of collectors who, with every sale, saw a whole new price structure for books introduced, the sale came to an end. The total value of the collection: $1,729,462.50 cents—nearly double the original estimates. It was almost an unqualified success. Almost. Because, as Jerry reflected, 'in some cases it seems I was carried away by my enthusiasm. It turned out that for a few books I had paid more than was realized at the sale. Even some Shakespeare volumes didn't fetch as much as I expected.'

The New York Times, in an editorial headed 'Bulls and Books', said: 'A lot of citizens having the means to gratify old desires or acquiring new ones, begin to "plunge" into the auction rooms. Not all their super-abundant treasure can be laid up in cars and diamonds. The immortal pleasures of the spirit beckon.' The newspaper had no doubts about why the sale had been so successful: 'In the first place with a minimum of advertising the Kern auction was most skilfully handled. Then the rapid spread of book collecting which is becoming a national hobby was an important factor. A third reason is found in the form of the Kern collection itself, with its carefully selected books and letters of high quality, many of them unique. Mr. Kern built a better mouse trap and attracted the most powerful competition in the world to his door. The magic of Kern unquestionably took its toll from many a surprised souvenir hunter who found himself paying dearly for the privilege of owning a book with the celebrated Kern label. Finally, and upon this reason all others are contingent, our era of prosperity was largely responsible for the huge success of the sale.'

The Wall Street Crash was but nine months away.

Jerry believed he was being particularly astute. He saw that a stock market that just seemed to go up, up and up might one day explode. Instead of speculating, he put his money into bank stock. But not all. The very morning after the sale, he found himself outside an antiquarian book shop and could not resist the magnet-like pull of the establishment. He went in, browsed around for a few minutes and then bought himself a book. The shelves at the Bronxville house were not empty for long. But he had started thinking about a new hobby. There was an incredible fascination in antique silver . . .

He also had his music to concern him, but that seemed to be working out all right. In September, he and Oscar had what looked like being a fair success at the Hammerstein Theatre with *Sweet Adeline*, a show presented by Oscar's uncle, Arthur Hammerstein. It was very much a family affair—the staging was by Reginald Hammerstein, Oscar's brother.

The Kern head cocked happily at most of the plans for the show. He walked in and out of the theatre, as always wearing either his loud shirts and slacks—which on him always looked impeccable—or his suits with the cuffs turned up and the silk ties, which to this day Betty Kern insists were his only affectation. He felt at home inside a theatre when things were going well. As he moved down the aisle to his place in the front orchestra seats, he was like a rooster surveying the hens inside his coop. But when things were wrong, it was more like a cockfight. While *Sweet Adeline* was in rehearsal, Jerry had effectively taken on the mantle of stage designer, director and choreographer as well as composer. As the scene was being set, the sound of his voice thundered through the auditorium, bouncing off the chandeliers and the rails of the balcony.

'The spittoon,' he yelled, 'the spittoon!' The show was set in New York in the days of Lillian Russell and Diamond Jim Brady and hansom cabs. Kern could not imagine a watering place of the period without its cuspidor.

'Yes,' said Oscar. 'You asked for the spittoon and we have one. It's over there.'

'I can see it is,' said Jerry curtly. 'But where's the rubber mat underneath it?' And he stormed down the aisle and onto the stage, looking for the missing mat. Without it, there would be no show.

The New York Times hailed the show when it opened as 'the first major success of the new season'. And the *Herald Tribune* said it was a 'gentle opera with appropriate music by Jerome Kern narrating a placid romance of old New York . . . one of the politest frolics of the year . . . a thoroughbred sugar bowl.' That sort of review was enough to make the ticket brokers frantic with worry. How would they ever get enough tickets? *Sweet Adeline* had practically all the makings of another *Show Boat*. Not quite all. But William Hammerstein was delighted. It was the first success he had had at his theatre, even though the first night ran at least 25 minutes too long—the curtain did not drop until 11.45.

Sweet Adeline—in which only 'Why Was I Born', sung enchantingly by Helen Morgan, who was as good as she had been in *Show Boat*, even approached the earlier standard—ran for a respectable 234 performances. But then it did have competition. The really big show of 1929 broke on October 29 and as usual *Variety* had a catchy headline for it: 'Wall Street Lays An Egg'. Some 16,400,000 shares tumbled in value that day and for a year or so almost no one would have the price of one of Jerry's rare books. He was lucky—until the banks closed and the near $2 million he invested after the sale, together with his other 'liquid' assets, vanished virtually into thin air. If it had not been for the silver which he had been buying as assiduously as though it came in leather-bound covers, he would have been ruined. He also still had the even more valuable asset of his talent.

For a time, however, no one knew whether the theatres would stay open—and if they did, whether anyone would have the money to invest in new shows. But as in all crises, the masses sought relief in escapism and the theatres did stay open and more shows were in demand. Though many of the men who had once backed new productions were now contemplating lining up at soup kitchens, if not jumping from skyscraper windows, Jerry was still in a position to take Eva and Betty to Europe.

Pick Yourself Up

IT WAS NOT JUST the Wall Street Crash which changed the entertainment scene as the Twenties gave way to a new decade. In Hollywood, the screen had found a voice and suddenly the word was out that the songwriters in particular might do worse than try their luck with the 'talkies'. Certainly, it seemed a tempting prospect. People could afford cinema seats where the price of 'live' theatre tickets was beyond them, and there were plenty of stories of former businessmen spending their days at the movies rather than tell their wives and families that they had no offices to go to.

In 1929, Jerry gave Hollywood a try. He didn't much like the town—it was too quiet for his sophisticated tastes; too artificial a place to contemplate as a home for Eva and Betty. It did, however, offer a potential market and Kern was never the sort of man to turn down that prospect. He was even talked into taking a small part in a film, but the experiment did not encourage him to extend his sphere of activities in that direction. It was probably fortunate for any potential director. Had he gone into acting, Jerome Kern would have been his own producer and director, and taken over the jobs of everyone else in the studio, too. He would have made them laugh—his wit would have devastated the screen writers—but he would have been anything but happy as a performer.

He was not sure, either, how much he enjoyed being a

composer for the movies. But he went into it gradually—and at the height of the Depression nothing could have pleased him more than the contracts he signed for film rights of *Show Boat*, *Sally* and *Sunny*. They were easy and uncomplicated. The first two used only the numbers he had previously written for Broadway, and the producers kept to their promises not to interfere with the way he liked to have his songs performed. In the third, he added one number which he called 'I Was Alone'. Films undoubtedly represented an interesting new medium and he was moderately excited by their potential.

He did not, however, enjoy the way Hollywood regarded itself as the only arbiter of what the public should or should not enjoy seeing. He worked for a month or more on the score of a new film for Warner Brothers called *The Man in the Sky*—only to see it released as *Men of the Sky* without any songs at all. Jerry was not one to accept that kind of treatment lightly. The producer's name was jotted down in Jerry's little black book as a man to avoid in future at all costs.

It was not the most glorious part of Kern's career, but like anyone who has had a fortune and seen a great part of it slip away, he was having to do things he might not previously have considered, and the cinema was an entirely new market that could not have appeared at a better time. Another indication of his changed circumstances was that for the first time in eight years he was writing songs to be interpolated into other people's shows. In the 1929 play by Dorothy and DuBose Heywood—DuBose would soon achieve world-wide fame as the writer of what became *Porgy and Bess*—Jerry had one song, 'Lonesome Walls', for which Heywood himself supplied the lyrics. In 1930, he wrote 'Anything May Happen Any Day' for the musical *Ripples*, starring Fred, Dorothy and Paula Stone. Graham John wrote the lyrics for this inconsequential number.

It all helped him pay his bills, although Jerry was hard up only by his own standards. He still found time—and money—for the odd book or piece of antique silver. One day he was standing outside a reputable New York silversmiths when he saw in the window a piece of silver that intrigued him. A notice by the side of the ornate plate read: 'Queen Anne'. Kern walked into the shop and demanded to see the manager—privately. 'That piece of silver you have in the window,' he told him, 'is definitely not Queen Anne.'

'I assure you, sir, that it is,' the man replied. 'Look at the hallmark.'

Jerry did not bother to look. 'I don't care what the hallmark says,' he roared. 'It is phoney. The piece is spurious and I demand that you take it off sale at once.'

The two men argued and finally Jerry revealed his identity. The fact that he was Jerome Kern was sufficient to ensure that the label was removed and the piece suitably reduced in price. He did not choose to buy it himself, although it *was* offered to him at what even he considered to be a bargain rate. He always knew what he was doing, and his judgement was usually confirmed by the appraisals of insurance firms securing his properties.

Kern did not allow the normal inconveniences of life to get in the way of his work—or of his play. Saturday afternoon was ballgame time and he had to go to the ballpark, no matter what. He would drive in his own car, and other motorists knew better than to get in his way. But on one particular Saturday afternoon Eva took his car because her own was being repaired. After fuming for a while, instead of simply calling for a taxi, he walked down the road to the nearest automobile dealer and bought himself a third car, an Essex. Fortunately for Jerry—who would probably have regarded wiring an electric plug as a complicated scientific operation—the controls were virtually the same as those on his other car, so he was not unduly perturbed at the prospect of driving the new vehicle to the ballpark. But whether the car rebelled at being handled by such a technical incompetent or whether it was simply a bad buy, Jerry's impetuousness was to cost him dearly until he finally decided that he and the Essex were not meant for each other.

In his way, he was equally impetuous when it came to writing songs. Once an idea was firmly rooted in his mind, he didn't care to lose it—like the time he and Oscar Hammerstein talked about writing a musical based on Donn Byrne's story *Messer Marco Polo*. Hammerstein was not as sure about the idea as Jerry. The score, he said, would not be nearly as easy to organize as, say, *Show Boat* had been—because *Show Boat* had been set in America's Deep South, a region where the folk music tradition was firmly entrenched. But, said Oscar:' Here

107

is a story set in China about an Italian and told by an Irishman. What kind of music are you going to write?'

Jerry didn't need to think about his answer. 'It'll be good Jewish music,' he replied. That didn't mean a sudden decision to go back to his own roots. According to Hammerstein in the introduction to the *Jerome Kern Song Book*, his idea was that 'there'll be no pretentious imitations of Verdi, Puccini or Italian street songs. There'll be no Irish jigs and there'll certainly be none of that phoney Chinese music played on black keys. It'll be my music, coming out of me, to interpret the story we are telling and it will be good.'

Unfortunately, good Jewish music wasn't enough to sustain the Marco Polo idea. The notion drifted and waned and both men went on to think about other things.

Florenz Ziegfeld, whose spectaculars were still showing as much of a curvaceous girl's anatomy as the laws of New York State allowed—and always with the utmost good taste—now decided that he wanted Kern and Hammerstein to write the score of his next show. It would, he said, star Evelyn Laye— the English actress who had caused something of a sensation in Noël Coward's *Bitter Sweet*. No title was divulged, no date was set for the opening, nor was the theatre named. Like Jerry's good Jewish music, the public were to be deprived of this, too. Anyone who knew anything about the way Ziegfeld operated would have known that making announcements of this kind was his favourite way of raising money. He was always broke and finding it increasingly difficult to persuade people to invest in his shows.

While he and Oscar were working out what they would do next, Jerry had the opportunity to work on another with Otto Harbach. He probably did not realize it at the time, but he was on the verge of the most productive period of his entire career—in quality if not quantity. Jerry was not the first choice for composer. Originally Sigmund Romberg had been retained for the show, but he had another project to work on and Harbach could see that there was no way he was going to be able to give the work his fullest attention.

'What if I ask Jerry Kern to take over?' Harbach somewhat bravely suggested to Romberg—who, much to his surprise, agreed.

It couldn't have come at a better moment for Jerry. Hollywood was far from a happy experience and he and Oscar still couldn't get a joint show into production. To quote Harbach, he 'went wild' about *The Cat and the Fiddle* from the moment the proposition was put to him.

Kern did all his work in less than two months—but those two months were crammed full with his usual pedantic attention to detail. In one scene, a banquet table had to be set with a candelabra bearing glass pendants, which were supposed to tinkle in a breeze drifting through a supposedly open window. Jerry was not satisfied that the tinkling would come at precisely the right moment, and in perfect synchronization with the music, until personally assured by the company electrician that it would. It took hours to arrange, but it was done.

Jerry was as fanatical as ever about the lyrics for his songs. When they worked, nothing would induce him to alter them. At one stage, producer Max Gordon timidly approached Jerry, saying: 'You know, I don't think our star can sing that line. Do you think you can change it?'

'I suggest,' said Jerry, 'that we change our star.'

When *The Cat and the Fiddle* opened at the Globe Theatre on October 15, 1931, with a cast that included George Metaxa and Bettina Hall, the *Herald Tribune* declared that it was 'one of the more painless of the light operas, having many of the blessings and few of the blights that accompany the drama's occasional interferences with music. As a concert, it is Jerome Kern in his most orchestral mood and as a play it is Otto Harbach rapt in utterances of some of the softest love bleats that he has ever murmured.'

It was also Jerry at his cheekiest. Otto Harbach had sold him on the idea of a love story set in Brussels, which practically gave Max Gordon a heart attack. The way he saw it, Europeans didn't fall in love, they simply had sex. 'Why don't we really shock him?' Jerry suggested to Harbach—who proceeded to write a real sex scene, the kind that would make an audience in Soho or 42nd Street feel they were getting their money's worth. Both men enjoyed Gordon's discomfort to the full before admitting that it was a hoax.

The Cat and the Fiddle was another Kern innovation in that it had no chorus. It was the biggest success on Broadway since

109

Show Boat, and contained a gem of a song that has to be included now in any medley of Kern tunes: 'She Didn't Say Yes'.

'Since Jerome Kern is not only a songwriter but a composer of music, they have made another attempt to break free of the stereotyped musical comedy patterns in *The Cat and the Fiddle*,' declared *The New York Times* after the opening night. 'It is a gallant attempt with considerable achievement and it gives Kern greater scope than he has had before. As a strong writer in good Times Square standing, he touches off a torch-song again. But he also writes tinkling ballads like "She Didn't Say Yes", serenades like "The Night Was Made For Love", a veritable score for a Pierrot ballet, to say nothing of a ravishing piano fugue. Among the Broadway slow slops, Mr. Kern is the man who is not afraid of hurdy-gurdy melodies and who demands something more than a thump and a squeal from his orchestra. *The Cat and the Fiddle* may not be his best score, but it is genuinely and infectiously romantic and a joy to the last piano note . . . The production is entrancing. *The Cat and the Fiddle* is not only good to hear, but good to see and as tasteful a production as the new season has disclosed.'

Brooks Atkinson added ecstatically: 'Not all the old flummery is out of this business yet. *The Cat and the Fiddle* has kept some of the old wine in some of the cracked old bottles and it has spilled some of the new wine in the making. But it has had the wisdom to put Mr. Kern's score foremost and it has, to a large degree, substituted beauty for the bromides of the trade. It is a boon to bored theatregoers, but it has something solid and fresh for those who hope to see the musical stage adopt the gold standard.'

Harbach certainly saw it as a triumph. Not only was there no chorus, there was no comedy either. If people could love a show simply for its story and its music—without comedians to laugh at or girls to drool over—a triumph it was indeed.

The show ran for 395 performances. In London, where it filled the Palace Theatre for almost as long, it was just as big a hit. 'In brief,' declared *The Times*, 'and with reservations here and there, a gay and easy entertainment . . . The opening is spirited and swift, enlivened by a preliminary hint of the evening's liveliest tune, "She Didn't Say Yes" . . . In sum, a pleasant evening.'

110

The lyrics were unashamedly sentimental, but it didn't matter. The music was smooth, lyrical and the kind that had those who saw the show remembering and whistling it affectionately for the rest of their lives.

Kern was not averse to a little whistling himself. The sound of a bird singing was one of the delights of his life, even though he usually spared himself the inconvenience of listening to the dawn chorus—unless as a prelude to bedtime. A bird's rhythmic song somehow always conjured up for him a happy image of the English countryside. Early in 1932, the sound of a finch outside his window seemed to spell out for him a melody that he couldn't wait to get off his piano and onto the nearest scrap of paper. The song it inspired became 'I've Told Every Little Star' which he and Oscar Hammerstein wrote for their next show, *Music in the Air*. Had it not been for Jerry's music, that production might have looked very much like any other German-inspired operetta—except that there was not much music coming out of Germany to match anything he was producing.

Actually, Jerry had become very good indeed at creating a German music form that fitted perfectly into the contemporary American theatre. At about this time, a prominent German producer wanted to use 'Twas Not Long Ago' for a new super-musical he was preparing in Berlin. He was told the stage rights were not available. 'It does not matter,' he said, 'it is a traditional German folk tune.' He really believed it was—until shown a copy of the sheet music of *Sweet Adeline*. He was not accusing Kern of plagiarism—he had no memory of the song before hearing it in the Broadway show, but it sounded so traditional that it was difficult to believe it could have originated anywhere but on the banks of the Rhine. Jerry was very fond of Germany and the Germans. But soon after this episode, his music was to be banned in that country, together with that of every other Jewish composer.

Music in the Air was another important musical for Kern, not simply because 'I've Told Every Little Star' became a great standard, nor because it spawned the number that could rightly be called Kern's own theme tune, 'The Song Is You'. The credits for *Music in the Air* read: 'Staged by Oscar Hammerstein II and Jerome Kern'—the first time in years in which he had taken second billing, but worth it just the same.

He took his new official duties quite as seriously as he had taken the unofficial ones—to the point of conducting all the auditions for the show. They took over the New Amsterdam Theatre for the purpose—which at the time was presenting the sensational Arthur Schwartz-Howard Dietz success for the Astaires, *The Band Wagon*. On the morning that, together with impresario Peggy Fears, they were trying out potential leading ladies, they sat listening to a beautiful girl called Katherine Carrington going through two or three numbers. They did not notice that Miss Carrington was being given frequent encouraging glances from the rehearsal pianist in the pit. As they sat in their orchestra seats discussing the various girls that they had tested, it was clear that the pianist was willing Katherine Carrington to get the part. Finally, Kern and Hammerstein told her that the role was indeed hers. Miss Carrington was ecstatic. After the formalities had been exchanged, she motioned to her pianist to join her. Turning to Jerry she said: 'Mr. Kern, I'd like you to meet my accompanist, Arthur Schwartz.'

Jerry was suitably impressed. After a few seconds of shaking his cocked head, he walked up to Schwartz and threw his arms around him. It was the best way he knew to show appreciation for a colleague's work. *The Band Wagon* was such an amazing success that he would have been very happy indeed to claim it as his own.

Music in the Air opened the night that Franklin D. Roosevelt swept into office, defeating both Herbert Hoover and the maxim that a sitting President never loses. These were strange times, and there was a desperate urge to be rid of the administration now held to blame for the Depression, Prohibition, and all the other evils that were making America a difficult place in which to live. *Music in the Air* seemed to offer a hopeful omen for the future. 'In the event that you hunger for a sweet story set to sweet music, you may gorge yourself to overflowing at the Alvin Theatre,' reported Percy Hammond in the *New York Herald Tribune*. The show, he said, 'is a honeypot of romance and melody whose only fault, perhaps, is that it is over-bountiful. This is a flaw concerning which it is not cordial to complain and I shall say no more about it. Mr. Hammerstein's fable is sentimentally Bavarian, Mr. Kern's lovely score harmonizes

112

with that benign mood.' Katherine Carrington's German maiden and Walter Slezak's village schoolmaster, he declared, 'are as pastoral as twin lambs frisking in the sun.'

Everybody seemed happy with the show, not least Mr. Schwartz and Miss Carrington, who were later to marry. The show provided what could well have been Jerry's own epitaph:

> *'The music's sweet*
> *The words are true*
> *The song is you.'*

Brooks Atkinson was to say that he took records from the show around with him on a world tour. Years later he recalled the opening night: '*Music in the Air* seemed to be the long-awaited emancipation of the musical theatre. For even in those days, people dreamed of a kind of musical drama that would dispense with the hackneyed mechanics of the genre.'

The audience found it difficult to decide which number they liked best, but 'The Song Is You' seemed to be the one they were humming most. Meanwhile, Jerome Kern was planning his next triumph, working usually in the solitary environment of his Bronxville study, scribbling notes on the top of the piano where Wagner still gave or withheld his approval. Sometimes Jerry worked on the card table which provided the atmosphere of the gaming tables that he found so irresistible.

As usual, he and Eva—with Betty in tow most of the time now—went round the capitals of the world, always stopping off in London for Jerry to go to the parties that he loved and for Eva to spend time with her family in Walton-on-Thames. Betty had grown very attached to her maternal grandparents, but her father's family she hardly knew at all. Jerry and his two brothers had drifted apart by now, and he rarely saw either of them. Being so self-contained, he never seemed to need the comfort that a broad family base brought to other people.

By now Betty's nurse had given way to a governess, the English-born Miss Maude Lydia Anell—a formidable, angular woman with a Wellingtonian nose that gave her the air of good breeding which Jerry thought so important. Miss Anell was retained to bring Betty up as an English lady (though she still attended a public school), and to teach her French, which she herself spoke with the finest accent Betty remembers having heard outside France. Although her manner gave the opposite impression, Miss Anell was a worldly woman who enjoyed her employer's music, but she was so undemonstrative that she would have hated him to know about it.

From the time that Miss Anell was appointed to the Kern household until Betty was 18, the girl never went out to parties or to meet other young people of her age without the governess acting as chaperon. A number of her contemporaries recall that Betty was treated so protectively that she was nicknamed 'the little Princess'—some say by Jerry. But Betty denies it emphatically. 'I never remember anyone calling me "the little Princess",' she says, rather indignantly. 'He was never as corny as that. I am afraid it is a myth.' Eva accepted Jerry's way of bringing up Betty as she accepted everything else about him.

Jerry was as fastidious about his clothes as he had ever been. No tailor would dream of making his suits with cuffs that did not button back; his shirtmakers, too, were aware of Kern's predilections—every one of his shirts had to fasten only to the waist. His shoes were always made by the same firm in England. Yet although he usually wore a hat when he went out, no firm could ever claim Jerome Kern as a regular customer. He never bought new hats. Whenever the opportunity for doing so presented itself, Jerry would beg, borrow—and sometimes steal —a hat from a friend, simply because he never thought they were comfortable until they had been well and truly worn in. He loved to dress up. When Walter Slezak saw the appreciative glances Jerry gave the costumes he wore in *Music in the Air*, he bought him a Bavarian outfit of his own, feathered hat and all, which Jerry tried on with great glee. It suited his extrovert nature to let the local citizenry know of his presence.

By now, he and Eva were beginning to commute between New York and Los Angeles—there was a movie version of *The Cat and the Fiddle* being made at MGM with Ramon Novarro, Frank Morgan and Jeanette MacDonald—and while he was working on pictures, the Kern family set up home at the Beverly Wilshire Hotel, then as now one of the most elegant establishments in the United States.

114

One evening after entertaining guests to dinner, Jerry dressed up in his Bavarian costume, wound a muffler tightly around his neck, jammed his hat firmly on his head and walked out onto the balcony. He waited for a car full of people to arrive in front of the hotel and then began to do what Eva always dreaded he might whenever they found themselves in a full elevator. For the benefit of the crowd below—it was growing bigger by the second, and traffic had come to a stop—Kern adopted once more his guise as a member of the Salvation Army, and began haranguing the city of Los Angeles about the dangers of alcohol.

Back home in New York, Jerry had new thoughts to occupy his time. He worked not just because there was a driving force inside him that would not let him stop, but also because he still needed cash to finance his mode of living. Not once did he ever embark on a score intending it to be a mere pot-boiler. He wanted to make money. He certainly also had ambitions to relive the glory that had come to him with *Show Boat*, and this was even more important to him than cash. *Show Boat* always meant far more to him than an outstandingly successful financial venture. In early 1932, he read a book that seemed to have the same potential as the Edna Ferber story.

His one-time partner DuBose Heyward had written a stunning tale, *Porgy*, about a crippled black beggar living in Charleston. The novel had been adapted by the Theatre Guild into a prize-winning play. Now Jerry saw it in a new light—as a spectacular musical. He also had a great star for the part, Al Jolson.

The thought of Jolson playing Porgy did not worry Heyward too much. The charisma of the man was virtually certain to make anything in which he appeared a box office smash. Recently, he had been appearing in films—the first talking picture, *The Jazz Singer*, in which he had starred, had appeared in 1927—but Jolson wasn't satisfied with his performances in movies, and indeed the screen Jolson was never more than a shadow of his real self. His magnetic reputation was essentially based on his 'live' performances as a blackface artist—so the new show would be both a great opportunity for Jolson to relive his old glories and for *Porgy* to get off the ground as a show.

Jolson himself was so excited by the project that he wrote to

Heyward offering to buy the stage rights himself. But Heyward was beginning to have doubts. George Gershwin had approached him with the idea of writing an opera based on the book, and that appealed to him more. It was, however, a long way off and Gershwin wrote him: 'I wouldn't want to stand in the way of your making some money with your property at the present time.'

It didn't happen, however. Jolson got involved in a new film and Jerry turned to another project. *Porgy* became *Porgy and Bess*, and George Gershwin created what was perhaps his greatest work.

Jerry had originally hoped to do his next show with Oscar Hammerstein—with whom he had discussed the *Porgy* idea—but Oscar was in London with other commitments and they could not arrange a mutually convenient time to get down to work. Instead, he joined forces with Otto Harbach on a play called *Gowns by Roberta*, based on a best-selling novel by Alice Duer Miller. It was about a couturier house. After barely a single performance at the try-out stage—during which time on principle something just had to be cut—the title was slashed by a third. *Gowns by Roberta* became simply *Roberta*. It was a notable show for a number of reasons, the best one being a song called 'Smoke Gets In Your Eyes'. It was undoubtedly Kern at his classic—and most profitable—best.

As usual, Kern took control of the casting, with producer Max Gordon having the final say—if, that is, Jerry didn't object too strongly to any of his decisions. Raymond (later to be known as Ray) Middleton was selected for one of the two male leads and a young radio comedian was chosen for the other one, having had a successful big-time vaudeville break at the Capitol Theatre. Gordon thought he might do well as the young man who falls in love with the house's top model. His name: Bob Hope.

There was also a saxophonist in the orchestra who spent most of his days trying to persuade his agent to get him a Hollywood contract. He was Fred MacMurray. There was a dancer called George Murphy and a sinister-looking fat man by the name of Sydney Greenstreet. The matriarchal owner of the couturier house was played by Fay Templeton, once the superbly beautiful Queen of Broadway but now heavy, ageing and unable to stand up for most of the show because of arthritis. Her part was curtailed so that she only played in the second act and all the time that she was on the stage, her 250lb rested on a chaise-longue. It was her last role after 50 years in the theatre.

The Ukrainian-born actress Tamara Drasin, who insisted on being known simply as Tamara, auditioned for the part of the emigré Russian princess who designed Madame Roberta's collection. She was given a private audition and asked to sing 'Smoke Gets In Your Eyes'. This was her big chance and she had difficulty fighting the butterflies that were competing with her vocal chords. Finally the number was over and she waited for the verdict of the men who were deciding her fate. Nothing was said. Now she became really worried. Kern and Gordon were alternately talking to each other and looking vaguely in her direction. But still they said nothing. Finally, she could stand it no longer. 'How was I?' she stammered, by now prepared for a thumbs-down and for another search for work.

'Oh,' said Jerry. 'You were all right. We were just wondering about that song.'

The song, as everyone now knows, was all right, too—except that it only stayed in *Roberta* because Jerry, hardened by his experiences in Hollywood, was determined to get his own way and keep it in. One actor had had the temerity to tell Jerry he didn't like it—'and that goes for a lot of us in the show. We think it slows everything up.' The director, Hassard Short, said he wasn't enamoured, either. Eventually, Jerry conceded one point. Perhaps the martial tempo which he had originally conceived for 'Smoke Gets In Your Eyes' should be much more relaxed. It turned out to be the way the world would get to know the tune.

In the days before big-scale hit parades, 'Smoke Gets In Your Eyes' became an instant best-seller. Within a week of the show's opening at the New Amsterdam Theatre on November 18, 1933, it was selling copies of sheet music by the thousand. 'It has,' said *The New York Times*, 'leaped to the forefront as the year's outstanding lament, a liquid delight to radio listeners and fox-trotting collegians.' More than that, the phrase 'smoke gets in your eyes' was being repeated all over America as the current 'in' expression. One writer, however, was to describe the song as the worst that Kern ever wrote. 'It wasn't Kern's fault,' said James B. Flanagan of the Cleveland *Plain Dealer* thirty years later, 'but that of radio and amateur singers of the 1934 era who played and sang the life out of it.'

But it was not the only hit of the show. Fay Templeton sang the haunting number 'Yesterdays' with possibly the feeling that only a woman at the very end of a once great career could muster. There was also a little thing called 'The Touch of Your Hand'.

Otto Harbach said of the *Roberta* score: 'His music was so simple in its construction and in its conversation-like rhythm that adapting words to it proved an elementary chore. A lyric like "Smoke Gets In Your Eyes" took me no time at all, so easily did the melodic flow adapt itself to the words.'

On the whole, *Roberta* needed Kern's music desperately. Harbach's libretto was weak, to put it mildly. Much of the production was little more than an elaborate fashion show which Ziegfeld would have done a lot better. And until the show actually played before a live audience, no one could tell how well anything worked. At least one song was eliminated from the show because there was not a single member of the company who, thought Kern, could do it justice. He and Harbach were tough taskmasters. Every time they appeared at a rehearsal, a cloud would settle over the singers and dancers. 'When they're here,' said one, loudly enough for the song-writers to hear, 'it means trouble. Something's going to have to be changed.'

Jerry could indeed be very inhibiting for any artist trying out in front of him. It was almost as if he regarded it as a presumption for someone to attempt to sing his songs without his personal blessing. But when he was pleased with an audition. his face usually creased into a Cheshire-cat-like smile. He always hated boisterous 'gang' songs, and if anyone attempted to sing one of his tunes in a tempo that was not strictly the one he himself had chosen, his reply was to stand up and leave the offending vocalist in no doubt that his days in the business were numbered.

While the show was being prepared for its first public performance, rehearsals were held with most of the cast at the Selwyn Theatre while the chorus rehearsed at the Lyric. He always walked into these rehearsals with an air of authority, believing that if people knew he expected to be the boss, there would be no question of his not getting his own way. But one day things couldn't have seemed more wrong. Instead of dancing melodically to his music, the chorus were kicking high and wiggling their pretty bottoms—things that didn't happen in a Kern show. There was so much down beat to the music that he couldn't even recognize it.

'For God's sake!' Jerry shouted, his voice rising to the balconies above the cacophony of the band. 'For God's sake, stop it! What's going on?'

With the deference that was always extended to him, he was led to a seat. 'Mr. Kern,' said the stage manager, 'I think you ought to take it easy for a minute.'

Normally, that would have been the signal for a new explosion from Jerry, but he became more composed and also just a little worried—now that he looked around, the theatre was not quite as familiar to him as he had thought. 'This *is* the Lyric?' he asked, rather sheepishly.

'No, Mr. Kern,' came the courteous reply. 'This is the Apollo. We are rehearsing George White's *Scandals.*'

Jerry politely doffed his aged hat, cleared his throat and, feeling extremely embarrassed, walked out into the street in search of the nearby Lyric.

It was beginning to be a good time again for people in the music business. Theatres were advertising for more dancers and musicians were being snapped up by the growing number of big dance bands—all of whom had a pretty hefty diet of Jerome Kern music. Economically, too, things seemed to be getting better and Kern, always a registered Republican, was heard to say more and more kind things about the new Democratic President—none of which he ever took back. Certainly, times were good for *Roberta*. Its run of 295 performances at the New Amsterdam was followed by a successful road company tour. At St. Louis, Missouri, 9,000 people watched a performance at an open-air theatre that began at midnight and lasted until three o'clock in the morning. Since 13,000 had attended the usual evening performance just before the midnight show, that meant that 22,000 people had seen it in the course of a few hours. It was the only way that the management could deal with the disappointed people who had had to go home when rain cancelled the show the previous evening. There was just time for the cast to have supper and take a few minutes' rest.

Plans were meanwhile going ahead for a new show. Kern and Hammerstein had an idea for a plot about three sisters; however, with this production they would reverse their normal procedure. Instead of opening on Broadway first, London would be the testing ground. They had what was arguably the world's finest theatre in which to conduct the 'experiment'—the Theatre Royal, Drury Lane. The output of Kern and Hammerstein had hardly reached the proportions that Oscar's partnership with Richard Rodgers would achieve ten years later, but the two of them—patrician composer and younger but no less gifted lyricist—went well together, possibly because both were perfectionists. They enjoyed each other's company, and, much more important, appreciated each other's work.

It was a convenient time to be in London. *Music in the Air* had just arrived at His Majesty's Theatre and Oscar had written to tell Jerry how pleased he was with the British production. Jerry never needed much persuasion to go to London, and the Kern family, with Miss Anell in attendance, soon arrived at Claridges—unannounced, and for once that was how Jerry wanted it. He intended to see *Music in the Air* for himself, without anyone being aware that he was in town. He wanted to see the same show that was presented to London theatregoers every night.

He and Eva bought their tickets at the box office and sat in the stalls, determined to react to the jokes and the songs like any other members of the audience. However, for Kern it was difficult. Instinctively he saw his work as though through a magnifying glass and heard his songs as though through ultra-sensitive earphones. But there was nothing wrong with the show he heard that night at His Majesty's—and he went backstage afterwards to congratulate the company on the way they had passed their examination.

While *Three Sisters* was being rehearsed at Drury Lane, Oscar was at the theatre nearly all day. But Jerry had something else on his mind. *Sweet Adeline* was about to become a film and he wanted to discuss it with Oscar—and Oscar was never available. 'I am now spending my time chasing Oscar in and out of Drury Lane and round about London trying to wheedle material out of him,' he told a reporter at this time. 'It is a case of the composer having to be content at the moment with the crumbs which fall from the librettist's table.'

Three Sisters opened at Drury Lane in May 1934, starring Charlotte Greenwood and featuring a fast-moving number that has long eclipsed the vehicle in which it first appeared. It was called 'I Won't Dance'. However, the motto of the London theatregoing public seemed to be 'I won't go'. *Three Sisters* lasted three weeks, and never moved onto Broadway, even though the *Daily Express* had commented after the first night: '*Three Sisters* at Drury Lane has the inestimable advantage of a musical score by the maestro Jerome Kern. When it comes to a score in music, "Jerry" Kern ranks with the Bradmans and the Ponsfords in cricket.'

Even if the show had been more successful in London, there was no guarantee that it would have satisfactorily crossed the Atlantic—for it was as cockney as a plate of jellied eels, and set on Derby Day. Audiences were warned to get to the theatre on time because 'the interest will commence immediately upon the rising of the curtain'. A real white horse trotted onto the stage in the opening minutes followed by flower girls, laughing policemen and a couple of on-the-course bookmakers. It had been intended to be a very ambitious production indeed, with the horse joined by a flock of sheep. However they had made so much noise bleating away during all the big numbers in rehearsal that they had had to be abandoned.

But there were even more important changes to be made to Kern's career. He had had more offers from Hollywood, and since that was undoubtedly where the money was, he was anxious to investigate them. He and Eva talked over the matter and as quickly as Jerry had previously decided to sell his library, they agreed that the time had come to go where the work was. They would sell up their Bronxville home and move to California.

Only Make Believe

JEROME KERN was on the verge of a new career. True, he had been involved in film-making for the best part of five years but before it had always been as an adjunct to his other work, a less serious (if more profitable) spin-off from his Broadway activities. Now, as one of the most prolific and successful of modern songwriters, he had made a decision that was to be among the most important of his professional life: he was not going to do any more Broadway shows for quite some time. Instead, he would concentrate on the movies.

It was an altogether logical decision. More people were spending time in the cinema than had ever gone to live theatre shows, and after a shaky start, the public now had a seemingly insatiable appetite for musicals. Economically, it made a lot of sense for him to turn his attention in that direction. Since more people went to see films, more would want to buy records and sheet music of songs they had first heard in the cinema. And because music from the movies was so popular, it was being played for twelve hours or more at a stretch on the radio. The royalties earned by Harms and Co. which were still providing the firm's joint head with a comfortable income, were each week proving the rationality of the proposition.

On January 27, 1935, Kern celebrated his 50th birthday and the entertainment industry celebrated it with him—in a radio programme; the kind of closely-planned yet spontaneous show that could never be repeated today because all the developments in sound and video recordings have made the hazards of that kind of live broadcasting not worth considering. Alexander Woollcott had decided to pay him a special tribute in his 'Town Crier' programme. An orchestra and a cast of celebrities were ready to help him—people like Noël Coward, Ethel Barrymore and Helen Morgan, all the big names of Broadway. The only condition was that it should be a surprise to Jerry. Really, it was a forerunner of the 'This Is Your Life' series, with Eva and Betty trying desperately hard not to let the head of the family in on the secret. The only trouble was—and Woollcott should have known better—it was virtually impossible to manipulate Jerome Kern and persuade him to do things he was not set on doing.

Two hours before the broadcast was due to begin, Jerry announced that he was going to pick up a friend who had just arrived in California from the East. Despite Eva's pleas, he put on his hat and coat and left the apartment. They were not the easiest two hours in Eva's life, but he did get back in time, if only just. When he returned with his guest, the radio was already switched on, much to Jerry's annoyance. 'Switch that thing off. I want to talk,' he said.

This time, however, Eva was insistent. 'No,' she said, 'leave it on. I want you to listen.' From the loudspeaker came the sound of his music. This was not unusual, and normally could be relied upon to put him in a good mood—after all, every playing meant an extra few cents in royalties. Then he heard Alexander Woollcott's voice pronouncing his name. 'Fifty years ago today,' said Woollcott, 'something happened in New York which, however little anyone suspected it at the time, was destined to add considerably to the enjoyment of existence on earth. Fifty years ago Jerome Kern came into the world with his head full of tunes and the world has been a pleasanter place on that account.' He then gave the bewildered Kern an order: 'You are to go out to your front door where a visitor will be waiting for you. Go yourself. Don't send anyone else.'

As the orchestra played 'Ol' Man River', a subdued, still bewildered Jerry went to the door. Outside, with a bouquet of flowers, stood Irving Berlin—who had been patiently listening for his cue in an adjoining apartment. Both men burst into tears as they hugged each other. Later, when the programme was over and he and Berlin were comfortably settled in the apartment sitting-room, all Jerry could say was: 'Isn't it wonderful to be eulogized while you're still alive to hear and enjoy it?'

He and Eva had bought a plot of land at North Whittier Drive in the heart of the most salubrious part of Beverly Hills and now from their suite at the Beverly Wilshire Hotel they supervised the building of a new home. Jerry combined the job of quantity surveyor with that of composer and musical director—in fact if not in name—of the Fox version of *Music in the Air*, which starred Gloria Swanson, John Boles and Al Shean. A number of songs were cut from the stage play but two more were added—a title song and 'We Belong Together'.

From Fox Jerry moved to RKO, which, because he had so many commissions from them, for a time seemed like Kern's home ground. His first picture, *I Dream Too Much* featured Henry Fonda in one of his first roles, as well as Lily Pons and Osgood Perkins. The picture had the first original Kern score actually to be used in a film—the *Men of the Sky* fiasco excluded. It was also the first time he worked with probably the most outstanding woman lyricist of all time, Dorothy Fields. With her, he wrote the title song 'I Dream Too Much', 'Jockey On The Carousel', 'I'm The Echo, You're The Song', and 'I Got Love'. He followed this with the title song for the Jean Harlow, William Powell, Franchot Tone picture for MGM, *Reckless*.

However, the big news was the film version of *Roberta* with a new cast, a new screenplay and a couple of new songs. RKO was the right studio for *Roberta*—or at least for the kind of version they wanted to produce. Under the production supervision of a dynamic young man called Pandro S. Berman, the studio had just had a huge hit with *The Gay Divorcee*, starring Fred Astaire and Ginger Rogers. It was the couple's second hit and followed on their tremendous success in the Irving Berlin musical *Flying Down To Rio*. And while *Gay Divorcee* was based on a Cole Porter score (only 'Night and Day' survived the transition of *Gay Divorce* on stage to *Gay Divorcee* on screen; the Hays Office, which supervised the morals of Hollywood's output, decided that no divorce could possibly be considered gay), it seemed only right that the next Astaire-Rogers picture should have music by Jerome Kern.

Once more Harbach wrote the script and most of the lyrics. But Dorothy Fields wrote the words for a new song which is now perhaps one of the best known of all Kern tunes, 'Lovely To Look At'. She also augmented the lyric that Oscar Hammerstein had written for one of the songs in *Three Sisters*. With Astaire and Rogers in a picture, Jerry's 'I Won't Dance' was too good to leave at the bottom of a pile of discarded sheet music. Nobody in America had heard it and not many could recall it in London, either. So there was no reason why it should not be resurrected.

Astaire took over the Bob Hope role but Ginger Rogers's part of a night club singer was largely invented for the film, to give her an opportunity to dance with Fred. Even so, neither of them got top billing. That was reserved for Irene Dunne in the part created on Broadway by Tamara, the Russian-princess-turned-designer. Helen Westley played Roberta and Randolph Scott was in the Raymond Middleton role.

The film had an air of luxury about it—not only were the cast powerful and the costumes superb, but the budget was $750,000, quite phenomenal for the early 1930s. Of the original score, 'Let's Begin', 'Yesterdays' and 'I'll Be Hard To Handle' survived, together with 'Smoke Gets In Your Eyes'. As background music, the musical director, Max Steiner, used 'Don't Ask Me Not To Sing', 'You're Devastating', and 'The Touch Of Your Hand'.

Pandro Berman left the music to the experts—except for 'Lovely To Look At'. 'It's a little short,' he told Jerry, with more audacity than any other Broadway producer. 'Do you think we could have it a little bit longer?' Kern gave Berman one of his studied looks. 'That,' he declared, 'is all I have to say.' 'Lovely To Look At' stayed short—but has lasted long.

There were other problems with Otto Harbach's lyrics. The studio worried, for instance, that the Hays Office wouldn't accept one of the lines in 'Let's Begin'. The girl who 'necked till she was wrecked' became, as a result, one who had 'no reason for vain regret'. But it pleased the audience and it satisfied Jerry Kern quite as much as it did Fred Astaire—who, if anything, was even more of a perfectionist than the composer.

Fred felt that there were distinct advantages in doing a

musical with a score that was basically already well known. 'When people knew we were going to dance to "Smoke Gets In Your Eyes",' he told me recently, 'they just flipped. We did it very slow.'

In *The New York Times*, André Sennwald wrote: 'With the excellent help of Professor Astaire, the Kubla Khans at RKO Radio have erected a bright and shimmering pleasure dome in *Roberta* which was unveiled with appropriate cheering at the Radio City Music Hall yesterday. The work is a model for urbanity in the musical films and Mr. Astaire, the debonair master of light comedy and the dance is the chief ornament. To watch him skipping on effortless cat's feet across a dance floor is to experience one of the major delights of the contemporary cinema . . . But *Roberta* contains additional splendours and delights even if the agile professor does create the illusion that he is always several miles ahead of his interference. Jerome Kern's songs, some of them borrowed from the stage edition and others composed for the occasion, are distinguished both for their literacy and their romantic wit. After being bombarded by the loudspeakers these many months, you may imagine that you are just a bit weary of having smoke blown in your eyes, but that superb lyric is still able to capture your attention. For the liquid sentimental songs like "Lovely To Look At", "Yesterdays" and "The Touch Of Your Hand" there is the cool soprano of Irene Dunne. For the pattering humour of "Let's Begin", "Hard To Handle" and "I Won't Dance", there are the extraordinarily pleasing dance duets of Mr. Astaire and Miss Rogers.' Sennwald even approved of the book. 'The libretto, which proved a definite handicap to *Roberta* on the stage has been visibly brightened,' he said, 'by the dialogue polishers in the studio.'

Pandro Berman for one asked Kern to be ready to do another film with Fred and Ginger, but before that could be put in motion, there were the obvious temptations of Jerry's remaining catalogue of shows that still had to be taken up. *Roberta* was followed by Warner Brothers' screen version of *Sweet Adeline*, again with Irene Dunne in the lead. She quite obviously enjoyed singing Kern songs. There were two new tunes for the film, 'We Were So Young' and 'Lonely Feet'. Jerry also retained 'Don't Ever Leave Me', 'Here Am I', 'Out Of The

Blue', 'The Sun About To Rise', 'Why Was I Born?' and 'Twas Not So Long Ago'.

The most momentous film decision as far as Jerry was concerned came from Universal, who announced another movie version of *Show Boat*—most people agreed that the 1929 film, revealing all the primitive problems of the early talkies, only underlined the need for a screen edition that did justice to the Kern-Hammerstein show. This time, the studio left no stone unturned. Not only did Paul Robeson sing his 'Ol' Man River' and 'I Still Suits Me'—with longer dialogue scenes, too—but Charles Winninger played Captain Andy and it was Helen Morgan as Julie who sat on the piano and sang about her 'Bill'. As though to prove that she and Jerome Kern were virtually inseparable in screen musicals these days, Irene Dunne played Magnolia and Allen Jones was Gaylord. And, as if to justify his position on the Universal payroll, Jerry added another new tune to the original score—'I Have The Room Above Her'.

The new film for Fred Astaire and Ginger Rogers was *Swing Time*. 'Freddie,' Jerry told Astaire, 'I'd rather have you sing my songs than anyone else.' And that was a compliment which in time would be echoed by both Berlin and Porter. Astaire's voice may have seemed light and without the range of other men who considered themselves professional singers, but he showed a respect for phrasing, for the melody and for pronouncing the words of lyrics usually only displayed by writers. Though better known as a dancer, Fred's singing was always a vital part of his professional performance—perhaps because he also wrote songs of his own. Astaire, Jerry felt, was not what he called an 'empty voice'.

But Jerry could find fault even with Fred, whose recording sessions he used to sit in on. After the first take of 'A Fine Romance' ('with no kisses'—something of an 'in' gag, for Fred was always being teased for never kissing Ginger because, it was said, his wife Phyllis was jealous), Jerry raised an eyebrow when Astaire mispronounced 'Arctic' as 'Artic'. Fred wouldn't have tolerated it either, had he realized, but it was Kern who spotted the error and insisted that Astaire re-record the number.

Again, his lyricist was Dorothy Fields, loving every moment

of working with a man she regarded as a genius, despite the minor flaws which only seemed to make him more attractive. She was plainly fascinated by his insistence on Wagner approving everything he wrote, and fell a willing victim to the charm and wit Jerry displayed at the small dinner parties he gave at the Beverly Wilshire for members of the Hollywood music colony.

Unlike Berlin, who had a reputation for 'never being one of the boys', Jerry enjoyed the company of other songwriters, and revelled in any opportunity to put forward ideas that, though they might be plainly ridiculous, made for stimulating conversation. At one party, for instance, discussing another composer, he said: 'He should carry on being uncommercial—there's a lot of money in it.' Anyone who didn't know Jerry well might have been amazed at some of the things he would say merely to provoke a good after-dinner argument. He was capable of assuming a stance that was totally in opposition to his real way of thinking. 'You know,' he would say, 'Louella Parsons is the greatest writer of our times'—and the hackles would rise. With apparent sincerity, he would plead the case for the introduction of lynch law, or for impeaching Franklin D. Roosevelt, whom in truth he was delighted to see win a landslide victory in the 1936 elections, and whose signed photograph was proudly displayed on his desk.

At one of these parties, provoked by Kern's reactionary views, Arthur Schwartz argued fiercely with him. Afterwards, he conveyed his dismay to Dorothy Fields. 'Didn't you know,' she asked 'that Jerry only said that to get the party going? He likes getting into arguments.'

On the other hand, if an intolerant remark came from one of his guests, Jerry then became the standard-bearer for all liberal thinking in the country. According to John Green, 'There could be 16 people at the dinner table but Jerry would be able to make a bum out of Cicero, Mark Antony and Abraham Lincoln at Gettysburg. Combined with that little cock of the head that he had, he would deliver scimitar blow after scimitar blow—but with much more grace than used to occur at the round table at the Algonquin with Dorothy Parker, Alexander Woollcott and those others who would lacerate people.' Kern's diatribes usually had their cutting edges only in their last complex sentence, and were frequently submerged in a flood of the longest words he knew. Says Green: 'He didn't castrate a guy but he sure as hell ended the argument.'

Working with him, too, could provoke the occasional argument. *Swing Time* called for Astaire to do the only black-face number of his career, a song that they had all agreed should be called 'Bojangles Of Harlem'. It worried Jerry slightly because the tempo called for was a lot more 'hot' than he was used to delivering. He had to be persuaded not just that he could do it, but in order to do it he had to reverse his usual life style. Dorothy liked working early in the morning and for her he agreed to start before his usual noon breakfast, and for her too, he for once took away the Wagner bust and replaced it with the large box of pencils he usually kept nearby. 'Wagner doesn't like me today,' he said innocently. He wasn't going to ask for trouble.

One sunny morning, she and Fred Astaire knocked on the door of the Beverly Wilshire apartment. Having been shown by the maid into Kern's room, Fred demonstrated the sort of number he thought 'Bojangles' should be. He did it in the way he knew best—by dancing from one room to the next, from the dining-room to the living-room and through the french doors onto the balcony. As Dorothy Fields has said: 'Jerry rarely had a feeling for a hot beat but after that he did in 'Bojangles Of Harlem'. It turned out to be one of the best numbers that Fred Astaire ever did.'

The teaming of Fields and Kern was the brainwave of Pandro Berman, who realized that the plots of the Astaire-Rogers films should never be allowed to get in the way of the music and the dancing. In *Swing Time*, it was a pedestrian tale of a dancing teacher—Ginger—trying to teach a man—Astaire —whom she just knows will never be able to dance. The outcome of the story was so predictable that it had to have good music to make it acceptable. Between them, the two writers achieved a succession of masterpieces: 'A Fine Romance' (which was sung as a duet by Fred and Ginger on two sides of a bathroom wall with Ginger sitting in the tub, her hair covered in shampoo bubbles), 'Waltz In Swingtime', 'Never Gonna Dance', 'Pick Yourself Up' (which became an Astaire classic that he has recorded over and over again), and 'The

Way You Look Tonight' which is perhaps the finest film tune Kern ever wote. It won him his first Oscar.

Even so, *Swing Time* was not quite the easy work that the seemingly effortless performance of Fred Astaire and the wondrous tunes of Kern indicate. Fred sometimes went through 40 takes before he was satisfied with a routine—once to the extent of making Ginger work so hard that her feet bled, turning her white satin slippers red. There were also problems with the title. It changed from *Never Gonna Dance* through *Swing Time* to *Stepping Toes* and then back to *Swing Time* again. As for Jerry's six tunes, they were all that remained of the 26 that he and Dorothy Fields had originally presented to Pandro Berman.

At first the results were not entirely appreciated. Frank S. Nugent had the temerity to write in *The New York Times*: 'After *Top Hat, Follow the Fleet* and the rest, it is a disappointment. Blame it primarily on the music. Jerome Kern has shadow-boxed with swing when he should have been trying to pick up a few companion pieces to "Smoke Gets In Your Eyes" and "I Won't Dance". Maybe we have no ear for music . . . but right now we could not even whistle a bar of "A Fine Romance" and that's about the catchiest and brightest melody in the show.'

Even George Gershwin presented a dissenting stance. In public he said what a marvellous film he thought it had been. In private, he told his close friend Mabel Schirmer: 'I don't think Kern has written any outstanding song hits. Of course, he never really was ideal for Astaire'. This, considering the hits that Jerry did produce in the picture, seems like a bad attack of sour grapes—or perhaps he had never forgiven Kern for not pardoning his failure to seek Kern's help for that first show.

When Jerry was not working at a studio, he was taking personal responsibility for the building of the house that very soon would be number 917 North Whittier Drive. As with everything else, he at once made himself the expert on building technique. The bricklayers and the stonemasons were treated to dissertations on the quality of materials to be used, the depth of pointing, the system of plumbing to be employed, and the speed with which he expected the job completed. He seemed to know as much about house building as he did about antique silver and books.

The house, built in French provincial style with white brick and black trim, was finally ready for the family, complete with Miss Anell and a devoted boxer dog that Jerry adored (even though he had to send his suit to the cleaners every time it snuggled up to him), to move in. Downstairs there was a living-room and dining-room and a breakfast-room near the kitchen, all furnished in Jerry's favourite colours of blue and green, together with what was quaintly called the 'help's quarters'. Upstairs, there were three bedrooms and three bathrooms and a sitting-room for Betty. Outside, he could look with pride at a landscaped garden and a pool. The centre of the house as far as Jerry was concerned, however, was his library. Like the living-room it was magnificently panelled, and there were pictures around the room of Noël Coward, Lord and Lady Mountbatten, and members of the Kern family, and there were not only books, but sheaves of manu-script paper in untidy piles on the floor—a situation that was never really to change.

This lack of tidiness seems to be the one contradiction in the Jerome Kern persona. True, he enjoyed dressing casually, but he never wore an open-neck shirt without his paisley scarf tied smartly underneath. He loved his outlandish shirts and just occasionally could be seen in shorts—but his appearance was always impeccable. Yet his working conditions were never less than chaotic.

When he built the Whittier Drive House, he did not think of providing himself with adequate storage facilities for his manuscripts, records and other tools of his trade. Instead, they were stacked in ever-growing piles in the library—and in the living-room, and in the basement, and frequently they over-flowed onto the basement stairs, and when he built a poker-room in the garden, they were there, too.

Jerry took personal charge of the the details of moving the household goods from Bronxville. He took particular care over his piano—a Bluthner model that he was convinced gave the sweetest sounds of any keyboard instrument he had ever heard. He had the best removal firm he could find because he always believed in getting experts to do work for him, and he knew he would never be satisfied with less than perfection. However, he decided he could not entrust his piano to a company more used to moving chests of crockery or suites of furniture. Instead, he arranged for the Steinway firm—which he was convinced was the finest piano organization in America and certainly the best-equipped to deal with problems like his—to move his cherished Bluthner.

As each piece of furniture was delivered, he and Eva happily supervised its careful removal from the truck and its loving installation in its new setting. Finally came the one item that he had been waiting for—his piano. The Bluthner appeared to be very carefully handled. He saw with satisfaction the smooth casing provided by the Steinway company. It was very firm. Everything had been not merely glued and nailed into position, but strongly screwed—too strongly, as it turned out. He watched anxiously as the removal men had difficulty in opening the lid of the packing case. It was not long before they realized why—the screws had gone right through the Bluthner's sounding board.

It was never difficult to make Jerome Kern angry. A wrong note could make him scream in a loud falsetto. An incorrect description of an antique would have him ringing up his lawyer. But now he was beyond anger. He turned white. Eva had to help him to a chair. Without his piano, he was without a future. Only that piano had made the right sounds. Irving Berlin had made a fortune and an international reputation by pounding out his tunes on the black notes of an upright piano that needed a 'gear' lever to change key for him, but Jerry's standards of perfection dictated that he must have a piano that was as pure as his music.

Jerry's pallor remained deathly. His pulse continued to race. Before long, there were pains in his chest. Eva sent him to bed and, for once, he didn't argue. A doctor was called, but Jerry was unconscious. He had had a massive heart attack. Twenty-one days later, the illness became a stroke. An embolism had paralysed his entire left side. For days, his family, friends and musical associates wondered whether this was the end of Jerome Kern, songwriter, but gradually he got better. A few weeks later, he was still having some difficulty in buttoning his right shirt cuff, but the paralysis had gone.

132

Jerry's recovery seemed to most people to be complete, but the fact had to be faced that for the first time since the death of his parents a serious problem had entered his life. Sometimes it made him feel morose, to the extent that he could not bear to hear of anything unpleasant. His phobia grew; if he sensed that something was wrong, he would turn to whoever was trying to give him the information and say: 'I don't want to hear it. Don't tell me.' His family and friends dared not tell him that George Gershwin was desperately ill with a brain tumour. When finally he did hear about it, he wrote Gershwin a letter—not realizing that his young colleague was already dead—'They have been keeping me in Cellophane and absorbent cotton and shielding me from all distressing news. So it was only yesterday that I heard of your troubles. I hasten to send you my best wishes for the speediest and completest recovery.' He was not told that George had died until much later, and seemingly from that time on Jerry was shielded from the merest suggestion of any unpleasant news.

Guy Bolton recalls going out for a drive one day when his car ran out of gas. 'Don't worry, Jerry,' he said, 'I'll go and get some gas and then we'll be able to carry on.' Jerry, he says, was deeply disturbed at the prospect of either walking all the way to a gas station or being left alone in the car at the side of the road. Guy made the trip to the gas station alone. By the time he got back to the car, his friend was gone. Jerry had hitched a lift from a passing motorist and gone home.

When Jerry went out in his own Rolls Royce, there was now a chauffeur to drive him. Once he took Harry Ruby for a ride in the car and they were involved in a crash. Had it not been a Rolls, they would probably all have been killed. As far as Jerry was concerned, it was yet another reason to distrust mechanical contraptions—especially in his state of health.

He was more concerned about being ill than ever before. For the first time, he now employed a masseur to give him a rubdown every afternoon—not out of affectation, but to tone up the formerly paralysed muscles. The masseur was Clint Hester, whom everyone nicknamed Willy and who became more of a friend and confidant than medical auxiliary. He used to talk to Jerry about his favourite hobby, coins. A powerful man with gentle hands, Hester was the Chairman of the American Numismatic Society. 'You know, Mr. Kern,' he said at one of their first sessions, 'you ought to get into coins, too.' The next day he brought in a few samples from his collection. Jerry no sooner saw them than he was hooked. 'You mean,' Jerry said, 'that a coin like that could be worth a thousand dollars?' He needed to hear no more. Within 24 hours, he had acquired a library on rare coins and before the week was out knew enough about stampings, dates and the various mints of the world to embark on a serious collection. From that point on, 'Willy' had to bring Jerry every book, pamphlet or thesis he could find on the subject. A little later on, Hester told another of his clients: 'The damndest thing is that he didn't know a George IV florin from a quarter when I first got him interested. Now he's the canniest coin buyer in the country.' It certainly was not long before he had one of the most valuable numismatic collections in the United States.

Jerry was once more playing the Bluthner—now repaired—and on it making noises that became hit songs. But he maintained that the instrument never sounded the same again. Some of his closest friends said that since his stroke Jerry was not playing so well, either. In fact, as the weeks and months wore on, his playing got much worse.

He still entertained lavishly, with Eva supervising these evenings for his friends with the impeccable taste that her husband demanded—even though she either felt left out of the stimulating conversation or was the butt of his wit. But the food she provided was marvellous.

'In his house it was always cordon bleu,' John Green, band leader, composer and now symphony conductor recalls. There was always a great bond between Green and the older Kern, whom he regarded as something of a father-figure. They had similar backgrounds, and Green wonders whether that was the reason for the rapport that they undoubtedly had. 'There are those who think that Jerry was an awful snob,' he says. 'God knows, it's true of me.' What Green remembers most fondly was the ritual that had to be gone through when he and his wife Bonnie arrived for dinner at Whittier Drive. The lady was not allowed to pass through the front door without first calling out loudly, 'Jerry'. Then Kern would run to fetch a footstool on which he climbed in order to kiss the cheek of the six-foot-tall Bonnie.

Jerry always called her husband 'Waldo'—never John, or as he was better known, Johnnie. Kern was something of a God-like figure to his 'Waldo', but there was, too, reciprocal respect between this man at the very peak of his career and the youngster on the threshold of his. Kern fostered the music branch of the Academy of Motion Picture Arts and Sciences and became its chairman. Green followed him in that role.

Another ritual was that 'Waldo' was expected to talk to Jerry in a phoney Yiddish accent. 'Zjerre,' he would say in the dialect, and Kern would screech in soprano delight. Jerry's own use of Yiddish was generally confined to an arid comment about a man's 'chutzpah' in trying to copy one of his songs, and Green says that he does not think he ever 'regretted not being steeped in his Judaic heritage, as I have . . . I think he had a pride in his heritage. I don't think he was very conscious of it.' If he ever did feel anything about it, it was during his time in California, when he mixed with an essentially Jewish group of people. Betty says: 'It was not until they went there that he and Oscar Hammerstein ever attended a Passover celebration.'

His religion was his music and his lifestyle—his enjoyment of elegance and his voracious appetite for having a good time. His craving for puzzles had developed to the point where he not only did the jigsaws and crosswords produced by other people, but made his own and had cards and pads specially printed for them. His most celebrated game was called 'Guggenheim', a test of wits. A player would put a category on top of the pad, composers, for instance, or cars. Another player would pick out a word from the dictionary. 'Back', perhaps, would mean a listing of a composer whose name began with 'B' followed by one with a first initial of 'A', and so on. He had also become addicted to poker and roulette. He used to tell Betty: 'You will never be any good at cards because you are not competitive enough.' As she says: 'I am now!' Above all, he seemed to love being the centre of attention.

He enjoyed going to fights at the Olympic Stadium every Friday night. Once, at the Dempsey-Firpo bout, he had the galling experience of bending down to put his hat under the seat and by the time he had straightened up, the fight was over.

However, the biggest excitement was going with other Hollywood celebrities to the Vine Street Brown Derby for a pre-match dinner. It was, John Green recalls, a meeting place for the famous of Hollywood, and one night when he and Bonnie joined Jerry and Eva there, Robert Taylor and Sigmund Romberg were also in the party.

Crowds of autograph hunters halted the traffic for two blocks, waiting for the handsome Taylor to leave the restaurant. With a small-check English cloth cap on his head and a muffler around his neck, Kern himself looked anything but a film personality, but with Taylor right behind him he was unable to make any headway through the crowds. A couple of books he was holding were speedily knocked to the ground by screaming girls. It was an extreme situation that demanded an extreme remedy. At the top of his high-pitched voice he began orating as though addressing a temperance rally. 'Savages!' he yelled at the stunned girls, almost bringing the traffic to a stop again. 'You heathens! Get out of our way!' The crowd fell back; it was one way of getting to the fight on time.

Unlike other practical jokers, Kern did not mind when the joke was turned on him. Dick Green—John's younger brother, who a few years later would marry Betty—knew this and took advantage of it. He and Jerry were lunching one day at a fashionable restaurant on Sunset Boulevard known as The Players. It was near Crescent Heights and is now a Japanese-style eating place, but at the time it was *the* local lunching establishment, owned by Preston Sturges, the actor-writer-director. Three women passed their table, one of whom had in tow a fluffy-haired poodle which Jerry, with his love of dogs, just could not resist petting. The dog fell instantly in love with Kern, its tail wagging so fast that it seemed in danger of falling off. Jerry kissed the dog affectionately. 'I wish,' he said, 'I wish I had one of these.'

Now Dick Green was a second assistant film director, one of the lowliest positions in the industry, the man who blows the whistle and has to organize the assembly of props—such as animals. In that capacity, he was very friendly with Rudy Weatherwax, the famous dog specialist who in his time trained both Rin-Tin-Tin and Lassie. After lunch, Dick had a word with Rudy, and the following Saturday morning a procession of station wagons drew up outside 917, North Whittier Drive. Out of the vans, 75 assorted dogs were released onto the lawns of the Kern property—75 dogs happily wagging 75 tails, each and every one of them trained to be friendly.

Eva screamed: 'Jer!'—the name she used when she was less than pleased—'look what's happened here. For God's sake get rid of these animals!' She was livid, but Jerry was like a small boy being given a treat. An hour later, the trainer called back with his convoy of station wagons, collected the deliriously excited dogs, cleared up the mess and apologised for the inconvenience caused by Mr. Green. But Jerry seemed to have enjoyed it most of all.

He was in general a sensitive man, and good music could move him to tears. One evening, the family were listening to a radio performance of one of Toscanini's many farewell concerts. Jerry was so affected by the occasion that the tears streamed down his cheeks. Betty, on the other hand, felt no emotion. 'Now can we put on some good music?' she asked. 'I think Daddy could almost have spanked me,' she told me.

Betty, growing up now, was still devoted to horses more than any other animal or music, and with the wide open Californian spaces available to her she was given every opportunity to indulge her passion. Jerry bought her a Gaelic gelding which she rode every day and which no one else was allowed to touch.

Jerry was as protective of her as ever, but at the age of 18 she was finally allowed to go to parties escorted by young men who had met with his reluctant approval, if perhaps not of his choosing. One of the first of these—shortly before his own marriage—was John Green. They would ride together and end up at the house for tea with Eva. To Betty, he says, her father was a potentate—'which must have been unhealthy'. Another suitor was Jerry's second cousin Charles Regensburg who used to meet the Kerns when they came to New York. 'I knew that Betty had been brought up in the English manner—which decreed that teenage girls did not go out with boys un-chaperoned,' he told me. 'But she was gay, fun to be with and very pretty.'

As might be expected, Jerry terrified the life out of some of Betty's boyfriends. There are hard-bitten Hollywood men who say they still bear the scars today. They recall him confronting them with his nose turned up and the question: 'Who is this fellow?'

The relationship between Jerry and his daughter developed from that of doting, over-protective father and little girl to one of artist and admiring critic. Betty would be used as the first testing ground for a new melody—a human version of the Wagner bust. If she liked what he had done, she had only to smile and he would smile with her. If there was no smile on her face, he would re-think the piece. Remembering those times, Betty says quite candidly: 'I'm surprised my mother liked me at all. She had every reason to be jealous of me. My father and I were terribly close. I was infinitely more close to him than I was to my mother.'

Jerry used to say to Betty: 'You know, you don't have an ounce of talent.' But he believed that there was one talent she did have—to understand his work. That was no small compliment. She also helped him with the intricacies of his electrical gadgets. He would never use an electric shaver because he hated the noise it made and it seemed too mechanical. 'Even a screwdriver gives me the cold chills,' he told her. Unlike other musicians, Jerry hated listening to records—of his own music and of other people's. He much preferred to turn on the radio or, better still, actually be present in a concert hall or theatre. Records—in the days when they were thick shellac discs revolving at 78 rpm—had to be changed much too frequently for his liking and he could never do it satisfactorily.

He had to weigh the disadvantages with another circumstance that always irritated him—the general lack of musical knowledge of his lyricists. 'Lyric writers,' he grumbled, 'are too lazy to learn to read music.' The only solution, he decided, was to have his own recording machine on which he could make permanent the sounds made by his own piano. But it was going to be Betty's job to operate it for him. Another reason why he chose the recording machine—a complicated system of valves, recording decks, pickups and discs (it was long before the days of tape)—was that he just hated repeating the same thing again and again to his lyric writer. 'Let him listen to the record instead,' he declared. Betty would have to turn the machine on, watch the dials and very carefully brush away the accumulated wax scrapings.

138

Eva was much more her husband's consort than his help-mate. One thing about her pleased him: she still spoke with a pronounced English accent. However, Jerry didn't appreciate her musical abilities. She had become a fairly good pianist herself but would never play when Jerry was around. His presence seemed to inhibit her. Occasionally at parties, Jerry would insist that they played a duet together, but she shied away from such things whenever she could. She enjoyed most of all playing Jerry's music, but was frightened to let him hear it. She was sweet and naive and allowed the husband she loved to rule her life to the point where she rarely did anything without his direct approval. That could be one reason why she chain-smoked.

Eva gained a great deal of pleasure from painting, preferring to copy the work of established artists, and developed a talent which she never previously realized she had. Jerry, however, would say: 'You can do better than that. Be original. Don't copy other people.' This, instead of encouraging her, inhibited her and she stopped painting all together.

It is possible that the staff at T. B. Harms felt much the same way when Kern was around, and that they greeted his removal to Beverly Hills with unmitigated relief. But if they thought the move meant that his interest in the publishing firm was at an end, they had another think coming. He had the accounts and all the papers sent to him by air mail and was constantly calling them on the telephone—still one of his favourite occupations. One friend still recalls a blistering conversation that he overheard between Jerry and Max Dreyfus, in which Kern insisted that his former mentor should work harder on publicizing a song, for their mutual benefit. Kern saw his music through all its stages—and the ultimate aim was to make money.

Keeping up with the music business included keeping an eye on what was happening to his own music. In 1937 he and two of his closest collaborators, Oscar Hammerstein and Otto Harbach, joined Irving Berlin in seeking to buy rights in the estate of Charles Dillingham. The kindly theatre mogul had died broke three years earlier and now the referee in bankruptcy was putting the rights to the shows that he represented under the hammer. The writers agreed to buy between them the production rights to all the Dillingham shows. The total price:

$10,500. And although they were primarily interested in protecting their own work, they became owners of the rights to some of the biggest plays in Broadway history—*Man and Superman*, *The Little Minister* and *Bulldog Drummond*—in addition to all the Dillingham shows for which they themselves had written. To succeed in the music business you needed to have more than a musical talent: business acumen, too, was a useful attribute.

Jerry's life in California—both professional and social—seemed to be working well. But as time went by, he grew less and less satisfied with it. Other top songwriters have found the same thing: Richard Rodgers was thoroughly disenchanted. It was said that the film town cut his partnership with Lorenz Hart 'to ribbons'. Oscar Hammerstein hated every moment there. Irving Berlin vowed to commute from New York to Los Angeles right from his earliest days working in films. Yet at first they all seemed to like it. George Gershwin wrote enthusiastically when he arrived: 'All the writingmen and tunesmiths get together in a way that is practically impossible in the East. I've seen a great deal of Irving Berlin and Jerome Kern at poker parties and dinners and the feeling around is very "gemutlich".' That feeling would pass as quickly for him as for many others, although both he and his brother settled in Beverly Hills and George was to die there. Towards the end of his life, however, it all seemed too provincial for him.

But there was more work in Hollywood than in the New York theatre, and it seemed sensible to stay where Jerry had built his home. He still liked playing cards and Hollywood certainly gave him his opportunities to do so, but rather like his piano playing, his standard had deteriorated. An open cheque book was always at his elbow—he knew he would have to use it. But he usually tried to recover. 'Just one more round,' he would say, 'for Russel Crouse's grandmother.' (Russel Crouse was a famous Broadway writer and impresario.) Nothing could persuade him to stop playing, although he once said: 'I think five or six hours in a smoke-filled room, struggling for existence against the aggressors, is perhaps a little arduous for this dilapidated chassis and weary, ancient bones.' His card games still went on well into the small hours—sometimes as late as 5 o'clock—though he did once thump the

140

green baize card table at 2 a.m. and announce to Betty, 'I am determined to have an early night tonight.'

Chances were that after a lost game he would go to the piano and work on a new song until daybreak. He made a particular point of doing so if he hadn't written much in the previous 24 hours. Even now no day could be allowed to pass without his producing something. 'That,' he once said, 'is a lesson some of today's so-called songwriters should learn.'

In 1937, he and Oscar Hammerstein did their first original project together in two years, the score for a Paramount picture starring Irene Dunne (yet again) and Randolph Scott and featuring a young lady who a short while later would be wearing a sarong and acting between Bing Crosby and Bob Hope. Her name was Dorothy Lamour. For the film, *High, Wide and Handsome*, Kern and Hammerstein wrote two of their great standards, 'Can I Forget You?' and 'Folks Who Live On The Hill'. They also had the distinct advantage of having Rouben Mamoulian direct the picture.

The same year saw another Kern/Dorothy Fields project, much less satisfactory than the previous one although their personal relationship still blossomed. *When You're In Love* for Columbia Pictures, starring Grace Moore and Cary Grant, was not notable for any musical landmarks. Both songs in the film—'Our Song' and 'Whistling Boy'—have long since been forgotten.

Yet Jerry was one of the few people who were happy working at Columbia Pictures, an outfit that was so lacking in prestige that at one time other studios used to threaten their contract performers with being 'lent out' to what was popularly known as 'Poverty Row'. One of the reasons was the uncouth behaviour of Harry Cohn, the iron dictator of the studios, who seemed to epitomize the Hollywood mogul at his worst. With Cohn, however, Jerry had an advantage. The studio boss was an ardent admirer of the greats of the musical theatre. A few years later, he would be the only studio head to show any interest in what came to be known as one of the biggest musical film triumphs of all time, *The Jolson Story*, because he had worshipped Al Jolson ever since he himself was a young song plugger. For the same reason, Jerome Kern was a name to be uttered in Cohn's presence only in the most hushed and reverential tones.

Other studios still sought out Jerry because his music not only developed and changed to suit altering tastes, but was enduring enough to withstand the vagaries of popular fancy. He never worried about the hit parade passing by for the simple reason that he knew he had always been musically above it. In all studios, in fact, Jerry got away with things for which other composers would long before have been shown the door. Again, his reputation had gone before him. Producers and directors knew that a man who could ruffle Ziegfeld or Dillingham was not be trifled with. And Jerry knew that he was bringing to the studios his own fastidious taste as well as his tantrums. He once told producer Sam Marx: 'You know, Sam, I'd like to write a score for you—but I won't do it till you stop biting your nails.'

Just as he made the rules at work, so it was Jerry who made the rules for his home. He would get up in the morning and stand in front of his small, elegant bar, rub his hands together and say to whichever guest was with him: 'Now, what shall we have? Let's make something exotic.' He was not a big drinker but he loved making cocktails to his own design because it was a creative act.

In New York he had loved dining at the Voisin restaurant, and still went there on his somewhat infrequent visits. In Los Angeles his favourite eating places were probably Perinos and Chasen's. Having the patronage of Jerome Kern, however, was never an unmitigated blessing for a restaurateur, for Jerry tended to treat his food in much the same way as he treated his collections. When Jerry was pleased with a dish he would insist on meeting the chef and asking for precise details of the ingredients and preparation—which not many restaurant owners relished. But Jerry usually got his way—and if he did not, the chances were that he would not patronize the establishment again.

An opinionated man, Kern expected his friends to seek his views before embarking on any major new scheme in their lives. To some fellow professionals like Guy Bolton he had become known as 'Herr Music Master', affecting a floppy black bow tie and declaiming on contemporary musical standards. But as always, he did not confine his views to music. When he heard that one of his chums had had the gall to build a house without consulting him, he was deeply offended, and he wrote and told him so. It all seemed good-humoured, but there was a germ of a feeling of having been slighted: 'Well, people will do these foolish things. I cannot understand it,' he wrote. 'Here am I untrammelled by any studio commitments, doing nothing except pitching and putting, quite eager and willing to contribute my expert services and yet in spite of it all, Eddie Chodovor buys himself a house, Eddie Knopf rebuilds himself a house, Frank Mandel buys himself a house; now you, without so much as a smidge of consultation with the master . . . This short-sightedness just forces me to confine my talents to the oil business.'

He was, however, still giving of his talents to the film business—although not as considerably as he might have wished. As his letter indicated, he was spending a great deal of his time on a pitch and putt course at Holmby Hills, playing with Harry Ruby, the songwriter-cum-baseball fanatic whose partnership with Bert Kalmar was to be the subject of the film, *Three Little Words*. Kern loved the company of people like Ruby and Gus Khan, with whom he also played. Both were products of Tin Pan Alley, and men with no pretensions. He also enjoyed pitching and putting—which took a lot less effort than serious golf and was much kinder to his hands, which after a day on a 'real' golf course, would frequently be badly chaffed.

Jerry needed time to devote to his collecting, not just the coins, but the antique silver and the books—in that order of priority. He was also a connoisseur of paintings and good furniture. When he acquired a Rhode Island 18th-century secretary desk, he was excited to discover that it was better than the one in the Metropolitan Museum in New York.

He devoted his attention, too, to charities. No cause received less than a generous donation from Kern. Today, Betty says that her father was 'charitable to a fault; a soft touch to everyone'. Certainly, the blind benefited from his contributions towards books in Braille. 'I can't imagine a worse affliction than being blind,' he said time and time again.

But he also found a lot of opportunites to write. In 1938, he worked on yet another Irene Dunne film, *The Joy of Living*, in which she co-starred with Douglas Fairbanks Jr. Again, it was a journeyman production that neither he nor Dorothy Fields had cause to remember with too much excitement.

Meanwhile, Jerry and Oscar Hammerstein were continually looking for ideas that would bring them, if not another *Show Boat*, then at least another *Music in the Air*. But they did not seem to be able to find the right formula. It was hard for Jerry; for Oscar, it was depressing in the extreme. He had had no success at all since his last Kern show.

In 1938, they tried—with the help of Otto Harbach—to adapt an original story by Edward Boykin called *Gentlemen Unafraid*, about three men at the start of the Revolutionary War—men 'unafraid' to fight the British and stand up for their convictions. The show was to be set almost completely at West Point and included a Hollywood-style montage intended to show the harrowing side of warfare. But the reaction of the Broadway impresarios was equally harrowing. The show had a 'world première' at the St. Louis Municipal Opera and died. But neither Jerry nor Oscar gave up hope.

Late in 1939, after seven years, they really had a show that was going to Broadway. . . .

144

Look for the Silver Lining

IT WAS 1939 AND JERRY'S MOOD was changing into one of anxiety—for a number of reasons; England, his beloved England, was engulfed in a new war with Germany, and while most Americans worried about the effect that this would have on their own country, he could only think of Eva's homeland. His equally beloved Betty had just married Dick Green, and with a father-daughter relationship as close as theirs, it could not have been easy for him to accept this new situation.

Finally, there was that little matter of the new Broadway show. It would be his first for more than six years and he was worried stiff—even though he thought he had written a fairly good score and Oscar seemed to be back on his best form. *Very Warm for May*, as the show was to be called, was to be both designed and directed by young Vincente Minnelli, later to become much better known as a film director and as the husband of Judy Garland. The rather light plot dealt with the transformation of an old barn into a summer theatre.

As usual, it was difficult for its writers to appraise their work realistically. Oscar liked most of it, except, that is, for a number called 'All The Things You Are' which he considered stood no chance whatsoever. Fortunately, it was allowed to remain in the score and is probably the very best of all the things Jerry ever wrote.

Betty told her father she liked the *Very Warm for May* music

145

immensely, but there was one number she didn't go for. 'All In Fun', she decided, was not right for the stage—and given her prerogative in such things, Jerry allowed her to argue. But 'All In Fun' stayed in the score, just the same.

When the show opened in Washington for its try-out, Betty and her husband went along for the first night. They were delighted. It seemed exciting, far ahead of its time, and likely to fill the selected Broadway theatre—the Alvin—for the rest of the season.

But show producers are never satisfied with first-night try-out reactions. Scenes had to be changed on the principle that shows were always changed on the road. By the time *Very Warm for May* reached Boston the critics were only lukewarm—the book had been emasculated, leaving only the still excellent score. By the time that the show finally reached the Alvin on November 17, the book had been changed so much that there was hardly anything left at all of the original story.

Betty remembers that Broadway first night very well. She had just got back to California, and was suffering from violent stomach pains. Her doctor diagnosed appendicitis which, he said, had to be operated on immediately—but she insisted on hearing how the show went first. That evening, the general opinion at the Alvin was that it had gone very well indeed, for the audience seemed to love everything about it—and Betty was immensely relieved to get her father's telephone call telling her it was going to be all right. She could go to the hospital the next day with an easy mind. When they heard about the operation, both Jerry and Eva flew back to the Coast instead of going by train. Both of them hated flying— though perhaps not as much as they hated the reviews of *Very Warm for May*.

Brooks Atkinson wrote in *The New York Times*: 'Out of respect for their immortal achievements in *Show Boat* and *Music in the Air*, Broadway is accustomed to bowing three times whenever [Kern's and Hammerstein's] names are mentioned. But it will be impossible to enshrine *Very Warm for May* in the same niche that does honour to their masterpieces. For the book is a singularly haphazard invention that throws the whole show out of focus and makes an appreciation of Mr. Kern's music almost a challenge. They have mounted it lavishly; they have also populated it with beguiling young people. But there has seldom been a book that fought entertainment as successfully as the story of this musical play. Although Vincente Minnelli, serving as designer, has adorned it with glorious colours and some splendid costumes, Mr. Minnelli serving as director has not resolved the confusion of the story. The direction sometimes throws away the point of the music. As is usually the case with aristocratic musical shows, a wealth of talent is represented backstage and on. But it seldom has a chance to put its best foot foremost. The plot scheme is against it; and the return of Mr. Kern and Mr. Hammerstein, which has long been anticipated, is not so hot in November with *Very Warm for May*.'

Time Magazine offered its only kind words about the show to Jerry: 'Kern's tunes were bright and strummy enough,' it said, 'but a raucous, epileptic plot made the show a bird that would sing but not fly.'

In his own book, *I Remember It Well*, Vincente Minnelli recalls how he attempted to turn those reviews to his advantage. He posted extracts from them outside the Alvin—but suitably edited to distort what the critics had actually written: 'they have mounted it lavishly . . . populated with beguiling young people . . . glorious colors and splendid costumes'. '*Time* Magazine: Kern's tunes . . . bright and strummy'. But not even these deceptions could save *Very Warm for May* beyond 59 performances.

Even though MGM bought an option on it, the failure of *Very Warm for May* affected Jerry as had no previous show that did not live up to its prospects. He returned to California to work on another picture with Dorothy Fields, *One Night in the Tropics*, starring Allan Jones and Abbott and Costello, the top comedy team of the period, usually hailed as the successors to Laurel and Hardy. It was perhaps a waste of a Jerome Kern score, though in truth it was hardly memorable.

The war in Europe was still uppermost in people's minds, and just as England was Jerry's main preoccupation, the fall of France had had a similar deep emotional effect on Oscar Hammerstein. Like all poets, he expressed his emotion in verse, and when he heard about Nazi troops marching down the Champs Elysées he poured out his heart in a poem called

'When I Last Saw Paris'. The first person to see this verse was his son Bill, a young man with ambitions to be a composer. Bill was visiting his father's Long Island home when Oscar persuaded him not to go back to New York that afternoon, but to stay for dinner. 'Stay,' he said, 'because I have something to show you.'

After dinner, Oscar disappeared upstairs and came down a little later on with his verse. It had nothing to do with anything else he was working on at the time; it was just pure inspiration. Oscar gave the verse to his son. 'Write a melody for it,' he said. 'But I'm going out to the Coast in four days and if you haven't finished it by then, I'll give it to Jerry to do instead.'

It was a formidable but very tempting proposition. 'There's only one thing,' said Bill, 'can I change that opening line to "The Last Time I Saw Paris"? I think it might be better.'

Oscar said 'Go ahead.' Bill wrote several melodies but when he handed them to his father they both had to confess that they thought Jerry would do a better job—if only he would accept the sort of working conditions which normally he would have rejected out of hand: there was no film or show in view, and he would also have to break his usual rule of never writing to lyrics—the words *always* had to follow the music.

To Oscar's great surprise Jerry did accept. Not to do so would be to turn down the chance to create a song that would do more for the Allied cause than a dozen newspaper stories and hours of propaganda films. What was more, it expressed Jerry's emotions just as it had Oscar's. The tune that Kern wrote brilliantly evoked the Paris both of them had known— complete with the sound of the taxi horns that Oscar described in his verse.

Its commercial effect was as electric as the emotional response it aroused. The first performance was by Kate Smith, who had had some experience with that sort of thing. She it was who two years earlier had first sung Irving Berlin's 'God Bless America'—the first time it had been sung in 20 years, that is; Berlin had written it originally for his World War One show *Yip Yip Yaphank*, but had abandoned it because, he said, 'it gilded the lily too much'. There were no such fears about 'The Last Time I Saw Paris'. It seemed right for everyone's mood— and the sales figures began to prove it.

The song was bought by MGM and included in their film version of Gershwin's *Lady Be Good*—which was now minus Fred Astaire and Ginger Rogers (they had decided to end their partnership), and starred instead Eleanor Powell and Robert Young. One result of its inclusion was a bitter row in the film industry, largely of Jerry's own making. The MGM publicists decided that nominating it for the coming Academy Awards ceremony would be the best possible advertisement for the film. If it won, the picture was guaranteed a long run, besides all the extra royalties that Jerry would pick up from the radio and its playing in dance halls.

The song was entered and it won. But Jerry was not happy with the Oscar that he and Hammerstein received. The Award, he said publicly, should have gone instead to Harold Arlen and Johnny Mercer, who were the runners-up with a little number from the film *Star-Spangled Rhythm*, called 'That Old Black Magic'. It was not mere modesty on Jerry's part; he realized that a principle was involved that could backfire on him one day: 'That Old Black Magic' had been written specially for the screen. 'The Last Time I Saw Paris' was not.

From his own point of view, it was ironical that the only song he had written in 40 years without a specific show or film in mind should be the one to now win him an Academy Award for film music. As a result of his protest as a senior Academy official, the rules were changed. Never again would a song be allowed to win the coveted Oscar unless it had been specially produced for the film in which it appeared.

Jerry was busier in movies now than he had been for a long time. He supervised an RKO version of *Sunny*, starring Anna Neagle and Ray Bolger, and MGM were still toying with the idea of making a movie out of *Very Warm for May*. He probably wanted that most of all, since it would at last vindicate his score. As it was, he had been lucky that 'All The Things You Are' had escaped from the straightjacket of its flop connection and was already established as a standard.

MGM, however, didn't like the treatment that they had been given by the writers and the producer who had been assigned the task, and decided to shelve it. Eventually, the project fell into the hands of a young producer called Jack Cummings who thought it had prospects. He had met Jerry at a party and impressed him with the way he played the game Guggenheim.

'Who are you?' asked Jerry.

'I work at the studio,' the young producer replied.

Kern asked him what he thought of the script.

'I don't think much of it as it is,' said Cummings. 'I don't think it's new enough.'

'You know what I'm going to do?' said Jerry. 'I'm going to ring the studio and suggest that you do it. We'll put this film right.' To a youngster like Jack Cummings those words were as musical as the score of *Very Warm for May*.

John Green was asked to make a recording of the tunes and vocalists were brought in to give it the full treatment. Cummings calculated that with Green's control of an orchestra coupled with all the latest recording techniques, he could not lose. He asked Jerry if he would like the recording brought over to Whittier Drive. 'No,' he said, 'I'll come over and hear it at your place.'

Jerry came and listened very intently to the girl vocalist singing 'All The Things You Are'. Cummings asked him what he thought. Jerry had a pensive look on his face but finally he came out with it: 'Why didn't she sing it as written? She changed the last note.' All that Cummings could say was: 'I'm sorry you are displeased.' What he did not know was that John Green had played Kern the records at Whittier Drive the day before. The whole thing was a typical Jerome Kern charade. The film never did come off, but a few years later Cummings's connection with Kern was to be cemented. He married Betty.

War had come to America now, but Jerry couldn't work up any hatred for the Japanese. The villains were still the Germans, but only because of what they had done to London and other parts of his adored England. Some people said he felt that way about Britain because there he could pretend to be a man he never was.

He still worked as hard as ever, and played as actively, too— turning now from coins to American stamps, which Betty helped organize for him. She put the specimens in the envelopes, handling each one with tweezers lest Jerry catch her damaging a find which he had studied quite as seriously as any of his

150

other enthusiasms. He knew all there was to know about stamps, and as might be expected, before long—working with agents—he had assembled one of the finest collections in the States.

Jerry believed Wagner still smiled on his music, but there was also a more influential group to supervise his interests. Ever since he had attended the dinner in 1914 that made him a charter member of ASCAP, he had been one of its staunchest supporters. Not only was ASCAP looking after the income of Jerome Kern, but also that of his publishing firm, which by now had become Chappell and Co. It was his—and almost every other composer's,—guardian angel.

By 1940, however, ASCAP had become a Hollywood-dominated conglomerate. The best music was going into films, which was where the best songwriters were anxious to put it. It was still the songs from the movies that were played on the radio. But there were changes in the wind. The gigantic rise in box office receipts that had come with the Depression and seemed to be established as the norm for all time, had halted, and there were signs that they might be slackening off and moving into a downward trend that would never recover. Radio, on the other hand, was attracting wider audiences than ever—and in America the staple diet of those audiences was popular music. ASCAP decided that its members were losing out. The only way to check the drift in their profits would be to demand a doubling of the licensing fee.

But it was not as easy as the Tin Pan Alley-Hollywood music men imagined. When ASCAP announced it was going to hold back on a new licence for 1941, the radio networks simply announced the formation of their own organization—BMI, Broadcasting Music Inc., which would look after the work of people who were not ASCAP members.

There was a great deal of scoffing among the ASCAP hierarchy, for it seemed highly likely that the radio networks would have to depend on songs that had long been out of copyright. ASCAP heads came to give pep talks to the studios, telling them that there was no way that their organizations could lose. Jerry was at the meeting held at Metro and joined in the cheering and clapping with the other members.

After the meeting, he bumped into his young friend who was

still trying to rescue *Very Warm for May*. 'You, Cummings,' he said. 'What do you think of this ASCAP thing?'

'Oh,' Cummings replied. 'Mr. Kern, I don't think you can win.'

'Why not?' asked Jerry. 'How long do you think people will be able to listen to "Jeanie With The Light Brown Hair"?'

It seemed a reasonable question because 'Jeanie' and the other Stephen Foster ballads seemed to be played on the radio more than any other old songs. But Cummings predicted correctly—BMI had a host of new writers ready to take up the slack. By the end of the year ASCAP had lost the battle and the songwriters were the sufferers—even 'The Last Time I Saw Paris' did not do as well then as it otherwise might have done.

Meanwhile there were problems for Jerry on a more personal level. *Very Warm for May* couldn't be turned into a film, and a new show he had written with Oscar Hammerstein and Otto Harbach called *Hay-Foot, Straw-Foot* failed to get a New York opening—the second time in three years that that had happened. Jerry had to content himself with seeing its world première at the Yale Glee Club, presented by the Yale Dramatic Association.

As if to fortify himself, in November 1941 Jerry donated a song to the nation: 'Abraham Lincoln Had Just One Country'. This, the second Kern song written without a special show in mind, was recorded on V-Discs and sent to soldiers, sailors, marines and airmen overseas. It had been written principally for the Defense Bonds campaign and was intended to be sung on the United States Treasury Department's radio programme. The master recording was made specially for Secretary Henry Morganthau, Junior. As Jerry said: 'I thought it was better to send him that than to send the song on paper. I hope the public like it as much as I do.' But there was a still greater departure from his normal work to come.

If Jerome Kern was a master of making popular music sound like an art form, it was partly because he had studied his business and worked at it so intently that many of his songs of the '40s were better than his tunes of the '20s. Unlike George Gershwin, he had no ambitions to write a concerto, a symphony or an opera. He knew what his kind of music was and generally stuck to his method of work. But 'The Last Time I Saw Paris, and 'Lincoln' had proved that there could be exceptions even to Kern's rules, and a year later, the conductor Artur Rodzinski suggested another change: 'I'd like you, sir,' he said, 'to considser producing a symphonic version of your *Show Boat* score. It is already a classic, beautiful music and American music, and I delight in it.'

It was a flattering enough invitation from the kind of man that Jerry had so greatly admired since his days at the New York College. But was it his 'thing'? Dr. Rodzinski had no doubt that it was. 'I do not see why,' he said, 'when it is considered appropriate to play waltzes by Johann Strauss at symphony concerts, the waltzes and other dance melodies and the songs such as "Ol' Man River" should not figure in an authoritative version in our symphonic progress.' As he said, it was the first performance of Gershwin's' Rhapsody In Blue' which put an end to the pigeon-holing of specific kinds of music. That was undoubtedly calculated to win Jerry to his side. There was also the point that if anyone were going to adapt Kern's music for the concert platform, it had better be Jerry himself. Rodzinski wanted the piece to last between 15 and 20 minutes in performance—but for ever as a part of America's musical heritage.

The New York Times greeted the suggestion warmly. 'This is a score which, by reason of its melodic inspiration, its workman-ship, its reflection of period and environment, has already won the position of a classic of its kind,' wrote Olin Downes in a long feature in the Sunday edition of the paper. 'It was created by a singularly gifted man, who had mastered his business for the popular theatre and its success has been richly deserved. There is a national as well as an individual voice in the music which should properly be given wide representation.'

When Jerry heard that Rodzinski intended featuring the projected symphonic poem (as it had now become) in his late 1941 season with the New York Philharmonic, he was over-come. He wrote to the conductor: 'May I try to express how honoured I am by your suggestion to include a version of *Show Boat* on one of your programmes in your New York Phil-harmonic season . . . For this, and the generous and amiable manner in which you present it, you have my grateful appreci-ation.' It was, although he did not say it in so many words, the crowning achievement of his career.

'In addressing an artist like yourself,' Kern wrote, 'there can be no chi-chi on my part and I cannot take advantage of your graceful allusion to the possible inroad the preparation of a concert version would make upon my time . . . The plain truth of the matter is that my activity in music over a longish period of years has been in a field far removed from the distinguished precincts of the concert hall, and I find myself unequipped with sufficient skill, technique or experience to create a symphonic arrangement of the melodies of *Show Boat* worthy of your baton.'

So he decided on a compromise. He did what he called a 'skeleton sketch'—which was, he said, 'about my speed'—and Russell Bennett arranged its final form. The symphonic poem was performed with the usual symphonic instrument line-up but with the specific addition of Jerry's own gift to the theatre —saxophones. He called the finished work 'Scenario for Orchestra on Themes from *Show Boat*'.

Its first performance at Carnegie Hall on October 23, 1941 was greeted by a capacity audience. Jerry sneaked into his place in the centre orchestra stalls just as the lights went down— but the musicians knew he was there. At the end of the evening, they tapped their instruments in applause—the traditional gesture of tribute to a composer.

Jerry was overwhelmed. 'I don't belong in Carnegie Hall,' he whispered to a proud Eva. 'But you know, this is the greatest thing that has ever happened to me.' And in the quiet comfort of his St. Regis Hotel suite later that night, he told admiring guests, 'The object of many of the older symphonies was to say as little as possible in the most grandiloquent, ponderous and intellectual possible forms. What I tried to do was to say as much as I could as briefly as I could.'

The work was not totally appreciated. The music critic John Briggs wrote: 'It is true that the work in its orchestral dress does not reveal marked individuality or what might be called "Kern traits"; one cannot help thinking that any good orchestral carpenter given the rich materials of *Show Boat* could have put together as solid a musical structure. Nevertheless the piece is a diverting one and might well merit frequent rehearings.'

Alas, it did not get those frequent 'rehearings'. Kern was, however, invited to do more of the same. The *Show Boat* poem was followed by a transcription for string quartet of 'All The Things You Are', 'The Way You Look Tonight', 'Smoke Gets In Your Eyes' and 'Yesterdays'. Then came another tone poem, written this time at the request of André Kostelanetz. It became Jerry's 'Mark Twain' suite—very much a labour of love, a tribute to the writer whom he read first in his life and who, later, had been one of his principal inspirations for *Show Boat*.

Jerry was as excited about the 'Mark Twain' idea as he had been about the 'Show Boat Scenario' and a lot less reserved. In a letter to Kostelanetz he wrote: 'All else is laid aside in my tremendous enthusiasm for our project which in the last 48 hours or so has left me well nigh breathless.' But even with the maestro and the Cincinnatti Symphony he was still concerned with detail. After the first performance, he telegraphed Kostelanetz: 'IN MY DELIGHT COMPLETELY FORGOT TO SUGGEST YOU RAISE BASS OF BAR 341 TO D SHARP WHICH SLIDES INTO E NATURAL AS BAR 35.'

If he was suddenly appreciating that his musical achievement could still be extended, he was not quite so encouraging to other writers who tried to bridge the two fields of popular and symphonic music. David Raksin, composer of the hit 'Laura' and of dozens of film scores, has less than affectionate memories of the time that Kern helped organize a concert at the Hollywood Bowl. Raksin arranged for Leopold Stokowski and John Green to conduct the orchestras at the Bowl and one of the pieces they chose was Raksin's own concert version of 'Laura'. Jerry did not approve at all—even though Stokowski had told him how good he thought it was.

'You are going to have to do another symphonic work, not that *little* piece you turned out,' Jerry told him. 'When the world has been telling you that a thing is good, it is very difficult not to believe it.' He was probably speaking at least partly from experience—though nobody would ever have dared talk to Jerome Kern like that.

Inevitably, people would ask him: 'Which is your own favourite song?' And Jerry always had the same answer: 'Can a father say which of his children he prefers?' But some fathers

155

can. and there was not much doubt that 'Ol' Man River' was his own favourite. After all, he still insisted on playing it whenever he was about to embark on a long journey and then again when he came back.

Not that he performed it well. Jerry's piano playing had not recovered from his stroke, although he didn't seem to believe it himself. He would still choose to entertain dinner guests with his performances—most of whom reacted politely, though one who did not pander to his vanity was Alfred Hitchcock. As Jerry played, Hitchcock talked, very quickly, very loudly and mostly about himself. His host finally had to admit defeat. He stopped playing, slammed down the piano lid and sulked.

There were times when Jerry could appear to be the most appreciative, generous of men. His cousin, Charles Regensburg, says that he was so generous that 'one had to be on one's guard not to admire something that he had—if you did, he would say that he would love you to have it. Once I admired a necktie he was wearing. He just undid it and gave it to me.' There was one occasion, however, when the tables were turned. Jerry admired a tie that Charles was wearing and said that he wanted one just like it himself. His young cousin combed New York until he found one. When he did, Kern wrote warmly to Charles and his wife Alice: 'Dear Alice and Charles: I am ever so grateful for your kindness in getting me the tie. Its welcome arrival climaxed a chapter of failure on my part, beginning with an unsuccessful quest at the Madison Avenue shop you recommended, right through ordering a silk square of the pattern from Charvet and two other lesser dealers. Since October, nothing happened with any of them—until you both came through so splendidly. With many thanks for your time, trouble and attentive thought, I am, with love from all, Affectionately yours, Jerry.'

Sometimes Jerry's generosity took totally unexpected turns, and like a lot of men with a reputation for being a martinet, he did not always enjoy his good deeds being publicised. When the arranger of one of his film scores was having a serious domestic problem, Jerry took a hand in the situation. The man's daughter, whom Jerry had known since her early child-hood, had run away from home and was believed to be working as a singer in cheap night clubs. Jerry discovered that she was in one of the towns where he was travelling, and persuaded her to return home.

To other friends' offspring, he did not always take quite so kindly. Once, Guy Bolton's daughter Peggy was invited to tea. She came with a pet monkey which, as Jerry sat at the piano, proceeded to bite one of his fingers as it was poised in mid air between keys. Neither girl nor monkey was welcome at North Whittier Drive again.

In her way, Eva was coming out of her shell. She had developed—no doubt through living in such a musical environment—a profound musical knowledge, and her ear for a potential hit tune was exceedingly good. She had got over her fear of the telephone now, and frequently when Jerry was out she would call a producer and say: 'Why don't you use . . . in your next picture?' She wasn't plugging one of Jerry's songs, but one by, perhaps, Johnny Mercer that she had just heard.

Mercer had recently had his first professional meeting with her husband. Columbia had asked Jerry to consider him as lyricist for the picture score. He was one of the bright young men of the music business, a lyricist who sometimes also wrote beautiful tunes, a musician who loved to sing his own material —and who frequently did, sometimes with the man who considered him his favourite songwriter, Bing Crosby.

Johnny's background was totally different from Kern's. Born in Savannah, Georgia, he was a country bumpkin to the sophisticated crowd with whom Jerry had grown up and done his early work. He was so absent-minded that he could not even remember his own telephone number. But he had a talent that Kern was quick to detect.

The film they were working on was to star Fred Astaire and the girl who was now one of the most glamorous figures in Hollywood, Rita Hayworth. Getting Jerry to work on a film was never harder. Before he would even entertain the idea, he had to know not only who would sing his songs, but who was writing the script and who was producing and directing the picture. He accepted *You Were Never Lovelier* because it seemed to meet all his requirements. He still liked to write songs for Fred Astaire more than for any other—and if Fred were happy with his co-star, then so was Kern. Louis F. Edelman, the producer, was a man whom he respected, so there were no problems in that line either. Especially since Harry Cohn had given his personal approval to all the arrangements—particularly for the director, William A. Seiter. But *You Were Never Lovelier* did offer a challenge that he turned down—one of the very few he rejected in the whole of his musical career.

It was Edelman who had bought the rights to an Argentinian film about a wealthy hotel owner and his four eligible daughters. He saw it as a great opportunity for the second teaming of Fred and Rita—who had been well matched in a picture the year before called *You'll Never Get Rich*, which had a score by Cole Porter. Fred will never admit such things, but Rita probably came nearest to his ideal dancing partner, tall (but not too tall), elegant, pretty, and with the kind of featherweight steps that made his own seem lighter than ever. With such a combination. the score to which they would dance was even more important than usual.

The problem was that its Latin-American locale meant music with a Latin beat. 'I don't write Spanish songs,' Jerry told Edelman as soon as the idea was first suggested to him. 'I don't write anything unless I can write it well and I can't write Spanish songs.' So the Latin-American medley at the beginning of the picture was not written by Kern. The rest of the picture's score might have found a place in any movie—providing, of course, it could have been made to fit in with the action in some way.

Jerry had spent his entire songwriting life going from one lyricist to another, so the actual process of 'breaking in' another words-man was not of itself traumatic. He just regarded it as part of the job, like opening the piano lid or getting himself a new sheaf of manuscript paper. The attitude of the lyricist, however, was far from being so relaxed, and Johnny Mercer, despite his earlier successes, was no exception. He was, as he has said since, 'awestruck but honoured' when Jerry first handed him a bundle of manuscripts and virtually instructed him to come back with some suitable verses.

When Mercer did return to Whittier Drive, it was with a number for Rita (or rather for Rita to mime while Nan Wynn sang). As Jerry sat on the piano stool in the library, reading through the lyrics of a tune they had decided to call 'I'm Old Fashioned', a smile creased his face. He didn't say anything at first. Instead, he called Eva to come in and join them. 'Eva,' he said, 'just wait till you hear this lyric.' He then croaked it in his high voice, jumped up from the piano stool and kissed Mercer's cheek. Eva beamed as Jerry hugged him as though he were a long-lost son.

Betty says today that Jerry always had a 'tremendous respect for Johnny Mercer—because he would always have half-a-dozen lyrics ready on time'. To say nothing of the fact that they were generally pretty good.

'I'm Old Fashioned' was just one of the big hits of the film. The title song, 'You Were Never Lovelier', was plainly another and so was the number that ran almost as a theme tune through the whole picture and was to become one of the huge successes of the 1943 musical scene, 'Dearly Beloved'—although in time that was to give Jerry a certain amount of trouble. A section of the song, it was suggested by musicologists of the period, was very reminiscent of 'Madame Butterfly'. Nobody suggested a plagiarism suit—although Puccini's death was still recent enough for the work to be in copyright—and Jerry shrugged off the complaints. He used to say he had a philosophy about plagiarism: 'Anything that is that close cannot be plagiarism. It must be coincidence. Anything that is plagiarized is whipped round so that it is not immediately noticeable.' It convinced some people.

But he never tried to sue anyone who had copied his material. 'If it's an out-and-out copy,' he told his lawyer, who once wanted to initiate proceedings, 'it must just be an accident.' Betty comments today: 'He never reacted as violently as I do. He was very fair-minded about it.' If parts of 'Dearly Beloved' did look too close to another piece of music for comfort, the whole tune was so sweet that even the purists did not complain too much.

One of Astaire's best numbers in the film was 'The Shorty George', typical of the fast tap-tap tunes that he just had to have as a solo simply because it was expected of him. But Jerry didn't like the film—and neither did Harry Cohn. 'Sorry, Jerry,' he told him after the first showing, 'but I'll make it up to you.'

By this time, Betty's marriage to Dick Green had come to an end and she had married a second time—this time bandleader

Artie Shaw, a man who did not always play the kind of music that Jerry liked. But if his daughter was happy, Jerry was, too. When she announced she was pregnant, Jerry was beside himself, hoping against hope that it would be a girl whom he could put on a pedestal similar to the one on which Betty herself had spent her childhood. Betty, however, said she wanted a boy, and indeed gave birth to one whom she called Steven Foster Shaw. It was the beginning of a relationship between grandfather and grandson that would be every bit as close as that between father and daughter.

Jerry now determined that Betty needed a good home of her own. She and Shaw selected a small house, but it was Jerry who took charge of remodelling it. It was wartime and materials were hard to come by, but Jerry decided he wanted it to be ornate and in particular have a great deal of black marble. He got it. In the end, his remodelling bill was much higher than the original purchase price. But it made him very happy, and the Shaws had good reason to be, too.

He was not nearly as pleased about an event 3,000 miles away on Broadway. American newspaper readers woke up one morning in 1943 to discover that a revolution had taken place that was quite as earthshattering as the one that in December 1927 had greeted the opening of *Show Boat*. And as in *Show Boat*, Oscar Hammerstein was one of the two main revolutionaries.

A couple of years earlier, Oscar had gone to Jerry with a proposition. The Theatre Guild had a play called *Green Grow the Lilacs*, and Hammerstein wanted to turn it into a musical. He thought it had a great deal of potential; it was strong enough, he believed, to give the firm of Kern and Hammerstein their first success since *Music in the Air* ten years before. Oscar was still concerned that although Jerry had had numerous successes himself since then, he had not, apart, that is, from 'The Last Time I Saw Paris'. He sent Jerry the play and a few days later asked him what he thought about it. 'It's a Western,' said Kern. 'I don't like it. Westerns don't make money. Besides, I object to the shivaree.'

He thought it immoral for a musical scene to be built around the idea of villagers joining a couple on their wedding night. In its way, that was typical of the thorough way in which Jerry

160

undertook his theatrical responsibilities. No matter how good he could make the songs, if he didn't like the story, that was the end of the matter. There was also that abiding weakness of the Western locale. 'Nobody,' he said, 'ever has any success on the stage with Westerns.'

Oscar Hammerstein regretfully accepted what Jerry said. But he didn't give up his ideas. Just as Jerry worked with other lyricists, there was no reason why Oscar could not work with another composer. Fortunately for him, this was the precise moment that Lorenz Hart broke up his partnership with Richard Rodgers. Rodgers and Hammerstein had a meeting, and decided to work on *Green Grow the Lilacs*.

Jerry anxiously followed their progress. He had reports sent to him on auditions and rehearsals. He heard about it all, from rehearsal to dress rehearsal and then to out-of-town opening. By then, they had a new title for the show: *Oklahoma!* As the weeks went by, friends detected a shade of green in Jerry's complexion. It became the principal dinner table topic. 'You don't think they'll make a success of this, do you?' he asked his guests and hosts alike, never quite managing to conceal his hope that perhaps it wouldn't work. When *Oklahoma!* proved a triumph, he sent Oscar and Richard Rodgers a warm note of congratulation. But there were plenty of people who knew how he really felt. Jerry was quite clearly jealous of *Oklahoma!*'s success, and said the score was 'condescending music'. It was almost—but not quite—the end of his writing association with Oscar Hammerstein.

There was talk of there being a direct swap: while Oscar was in partnership with Rodgers, Lorenz Hart would work with Jerry. But for a number of reasons, that never came off; Hart didn't want to move to California, and in any case, he was suffering badly from the effects of the alcoholism and depression that were soon to kill him. I doubt, too, that Jerry would have appreciated a man whom he possibly now regarded as a 'cast off'.

Jerry had never been prepared to allow the life of any of his shows or songs to be limited to the time in which they were written, and in 1943 a Kern show opened in London that cheered many a depressed family suffering from the effects of bombing and wartime deprivations. Jessie Matthews, star of pre-war London shows and of early British film musicals, headed the cast of *Wild Rose* which to anyone familiar with what had gone before could easily recognize as *Sally* wearing a wartime Utility dress. Since this was the first real theatrical experience of my life, I remember it with particular affection. Sitting at the back of the stalls listening to Jessie Matthews singing 'Look For The Silver Lining' is a memory that will never leave me.

The Times, too, was impressed—if not quite as much as I was on that holiday from my primary school. 'Mr. Firth Shephard [the producer] has given wartime London some lively musical entertainments,' said its anonymous critic, 'this is the least sophisticated of them all but not the least pleasing.'

Eva's parents had both died. Mr. Leale had forecast the exact date of his death—and was only 30 years out in his prediction. For those extra 30 years, Jerry had been keeping both of his parents-in-law in a manner to which they had become accustomed. At the age of 59, Jerry had no thought of living any other way himself. In 1944, his talent was still in great demand, and the Hollywood studios were still paying vast sums for it.

For Universal he wrote an original score for a Deanna Durbin picture called *Can't Help Singing*; once more the income from the title song alone would have kept the average man very content indeed for the next few years. Also notable in the score were 'More and More', 'Any Moment Now' and 'Californi-ay,' all with lyrics by E.Y. (Yip) Harburg.

He followed that movie with one of his biggest film commissions to date—another Rita Hayworth picture for Columbia, and one that has since come to be regarded as the archetypal glamour movie: *Cover Girl*. It also featured an up-and-coming young dancer called Gene Kelly.

The reason Jerry came to write the score was due to that other songwriter, Arthur Schwartz. Some five years earlier, Schwartz had collaborated on a script he called *A Young Girl's Fancy*. It was written with Jean Arthur in mind and then sold to Columbia. The movie was never made and Schwartz tried to buy back the rights from the studio so that he could use the story for a stage show starring a girl called Zarina. He talked to Harry Cohn about it in his suite at the Sherry Netherland

162

Hotel in New York, but Cohn had other ideas.

'I like your work,' said the mogul. 'How would you like to be the producer of the new Rita Hayworth film, *Cover Girl*?'

Schwartz protested that Cohn must have the wrong guy. He had never produced a film in his life. But the studio head was insistent. 'That doesn't matter,' he said, 'and I want you to write the score, too.'

Schwartz liked the idea, particularly playing producer. But he said: 'I couldn't write the score *and* learn how to be a producer. I'll get someone else.'

'Who'll you get?' asked Cohn, puffing his cigar anxiously.

'I'll get the best—Jerry Kern.'

The suggestion appealed to both Cohn and Kern. To the studio head, it represented a chance to make up to Jerry for *You Were Never Lovelier*. They both also liked the proposition that Jerry should have yet another new lyricist, this time a man universally recognized as one of the very best—George Gershwin's elder brother, Ira. By all accounts, they enjoyed working·together, with Jerry reclining on a leather couch while Ira sang his lines to the composer from a foot-stool at his side. Even with this acknowledged master of words, Jerry still made it clear that it would be *his* score and that he was the chief. And a very fussy one at that, insisting on the usual 55–45 percent share of royalties in his favour.

He and Gershwin finished a number for Gene Kelly called 'Put Me To The Test', a rhythm song which put the full focus on the dancer in a film that, unusually for the time, had no great big Busby Berkeley-type choruses.

'What d'ya think of it?' Jerry asked when Arthur Schwartz popped in to watch the first rehearsal.

'It's fine,' said the producer, clearly registering no great signs of enthusiasm. When Jerry saw that, he left the room.

A couple of days later, Schwartz had a telephone call from his disappointed composer: 'About that song, "Put Me To The Test",' he said, and there was an angry edge to his voice. 'Look, I'm now up at Metro for another film and if you don't like it, I'll use it here.'

Schwartz was thoroughly taken aback. 'Jerry,' he replied, 'it's up to you . . . but I think it's very practical for what we have in mind . . .'

163

Jerry didn't let him finish his sentence. 'I have a feeling you don't like it,' he said, 'and don't want to do anything with it.'

'No,' the producer protested. 'I like it. But I think my idea of its value outside the film is a little different from yours.'

For a time, there was a distinct coolness—bordering on unpleasantness—between them, simply because Schwartz had had the temerity to speak his mind and express a tiny doubt about the master's work. But when the difficulties were smoothed over Jerry was less scratchy. He was also back to his old witty self—even if, as Schwartz suspected, he was 'borrowing' from another composer. A few bars of his song 'Who's Complaining?' was, says the producer, a direct crib from Noël Coward's 'Mad Dogs And Englishmen'. 'Jerry,' Schwartz told him, 'you can't use that. It's from Noël Coward.'

'I know,' Kern replied. 'But I'm not stealing. I'm just quoting.'

Arthur even had the courage to suggest that he might have done it before—in his *Swing Time* song, 'Pick Yourself Up'—which, he said, contained an extract from the opera *Schwanda*. Jerry only smiled. Now Schwartz says: 'Most "steals" are known by the people doing it. But Jerry Kern was never like Romberg, about whom they used to say "he writes music of the kind you whistle going *into* the theatre".'

Thereafter, whenever he and his producer had any differences of opinion over a song, Jerry marked the manuscript 'ADL'—standing for 'Arthur Doesn't Like'.

Arthur plainly did like the big song from *Cover Girl*, 'Long Ago And Far Away'. When a songwriter approaching his 60th birthday can produce tunes like 'Long Ago', it is easy to understand the awe in which he is held—particularly by others in his business.

Richard Rodgers was never one of the Kern set, although he always said how much he admired Jerry and how great Kern's influence on his own work had been. In 1944, he tried several times to get an appointment to meet him—but, as he has said in his autobiography, he always sensed that Eva was trying to protect her husband and keep outsiders away. Yet when they did eventually meet, the two men from different generations but a similar world chatted amiably enough by Jerry's swimming pool.

Jule Styne, then still in his thirties, was similarly reverential about Kern's name. For years, he has been regaling song-writing friends with the story of how he finally made it—after being terribly hurt that Jerry never included him in his regular Sunday night dinner parties. (Jerry had four or five circles of friends and these dinners were ways of seeing them all. But his popularity did bring problems. When they wanted to celebrate their wedding anniversary he and Eva used to leave town— because there was no way of entertaining everyone under one roof.) When the invitation eventually came, Styne was ecstatic. And the evening was made even more splendid when Jerry button-holed him at the end of the party and said: 'I'd like you to come over for breakfast tomorrow.'

As Arthur Schwartz recalls: 'Jule was overjoyed. Alone with Kern for breakfast!' The next day, bright and elevenish, Styne was at North Whittier Drive. The maid showed him in and Jerry was as usual the perfect host. But all the time that they were eating, Styne was wondering what it was all about— for so far there had been no flattering comments about his work, no requests for help on a new score, no amusing gossip about mutual colleagues. Finally, however, all was revealed. 'I was wondering . . .' Jerry said pensively. 'I understand, Jule, that you do a lot of betting at the race track and wonder if you have any good tips for me?'

It sounded a lot funnier when he told the story to a group of assembled ASCAP members several years later than it did that morning at North Whittier Drive. Jerry doubtless always had the excuse that he was too preoccupied with his own work to think about the feelings of people such as lyricists, whom he always tended to regard as lesser mortals.

He wrote a song with Yip Harburg for the MGM film *Song of Russia* called 'And Russia Is Her Name'. It was the time when relations between America and the Soviet Union were at their sweetest and even Jerry was willing to go along with this. It seemed the patriotic thing to do. As a gesture of appreciation of that patriotism and of Jerry's contribution to American culture, he was elected a member of the National Institute of Arts and Letters. But that didn't make him any easier to work with.

Leo Robin, the lyricist known in Hollywood as 'the poet'—

he had created the Bob Hope-Shirley Ross classic 'Thanks For The Memory'—was assigned to work with Kern on a film for Twentieth Century Fox called *Centennial Summer*, and has frequently been heard to say since that he wished he had not been. For the combination of Kern and Robin was far from ideal.

Jerry of course always liked perfection, but to his own prescription. Robin enjoyed taking his time over things—six weeks over one lyric if that were the only way to get it done properly. After those weeks of waiting for one number from the score that Jerry wanted to call 'All Through The Day', the meeting between Kern and Robin was stormy. In the end, Jerry brought in Oscar Hammerstein to do the lyric—although Robin had already produced 'In Love In Vain', 'Cinderella Sue,' 'Up With The Lark' and 'Two Hearts Are Better Than One'.

The trouble stemmed from Kern's refusal to accept Robin as an equal partner. He would, as usual, scribble his dummy lyrics and give the lyricist the pile of manuscripts to work on. 'We never socialized in any way,' Robin told me. 'But I was always very correct with him. The music stayed exactly the way he wrote it.'

Just one lyric stayed the way Jerry wrote it, too. Betty had been reading a book by Michael Fessier called *Fully Dressed and in My Right Mind*. She adored it. Afterwards, it became the title of a song her father wrote for her—although it was never published.

A new film planned by MGM was to have much wider exposure. It was called *Till the Clouds Roll By*. Hollywood had come to terms with the fact that there was no better way to get a perfectly tried musical score into a movie than by featuring the collected works of a single composer. Jerry's life, MGM decided, must have all the ingredients of a good story, together with the sort of music everyone knew and everyone loved. Unlike Irving Berlin, who would never allow his life story to be told on film in any way (as a result at least four fictitious films were devoted to music he had written over the length of his amazing career), Jerry was flattered by the Metro proposal. 'But,' he told Louis B. Mayer, 'you mustn't try to tell my life story. You'd find it all far too dull. Make up a story and

166

everyone'll be happy—so long as you play my music the way that I wrote it.'

The man assigned to pen the story was Jerry's old friend, professional partner and sometime adversary, Guy Bolton, who managed to drag a compromise from his subiect. He could not only use his music, but could take as the picture's theme the true story of how Jerry helped a friend find his long-lost daughter. The friend had been a very cultured Englishman, and Jerry had often spoken of the tremendous influence he had had on his own early years. There was, Bolton decided, certainly the germ of a plot there—although what he really wanted to do was to describe Jerry's relationship with Betty. Kern wouldn't have that.

Betty now says she finds it difficult to understand why her father sanctioned the film at all. 'But my mother was very grateful,' she told me, 'that it wasn't worse.' Of course, it did make a lot of money for the Kern estate. The story was dragged way beyond the bounds either of truth or probability, but the music was as true as it was real. It included most of Jerry's best numbers, ranging from 'How'd You Like To Spoon With Me?' to the 'Mark Twain Suite' and featuring in the process 'Why Was I Born?', 'Smoke Gets In Your Eyes', 'All The Things You Are', 'Long Ago And Far Away', 'Look For The Silver Lining' and 15 others, culminating with a young, frail-looking Frank Sinatra standing on a heavenly staircase and singing 'Ol' Man River'. An impossibly young, handsome Robert Walker played Kern—bearing no more resemblance to him than did most of the story to his life.

As always, Jerry had had his own ideas about casting. 'Burgess Meredith,' he suggested, 'now there's a young man who would play me very well.' But the producers didn't agree and Walker was cast instead. Eva was played by Dorothy Patrick, who bore as much resemblance to Mrs. Kern, as Robert Walker did to her husband.

What no one knew when the contracts were signed and filming began was that it would serve as an instant memorial.

Land Where the Good Songs Go

THE WORLD HAD CHANGED, and Jerry saw no reason to be dissatisfied with it. *Till the Clouds Roll By* was a tribute he could not fail to appreciate. Better still, his beloved England had come through the war, scarred but free, and the world was at peace again—even though he told Betty he suspected that the atomic bomb had never been dropped at all, but was simply a face-saving propaganda device to allow the Japanese to surrender.

What made him happiest of all, however, was that Oscar Hammerstein had presented him with two very good reasons to go to New York—one, a revival of *Show Boat,* the second an invitation to write a big new Broadway show. For a man of his age, both were enticing but worrying opportunities. Although he felt as much in demand now as he had when Bessie Marbury first suggested he write a show for a little theatre called the Princess, understandably, the notion of competing in the post-*Oklahoma!* age was a daunting one. He had not had a new Broadway play since *Very Warm for May,* and the thought of going through the traumas of that again made him shudder with anxiety. On the other hand, it *was* what he had always wanted.

The *Show Boat* revival was thrilling enough—for the first time in 12 years Broadway audiences would have the chance of reliving one of the magic moments in American theatrical history, and a new generation, too, would see for themselves what all the fuss had been about.

After the tremendous success of *Oklahoma!* and then *Carousel*, Rodgers and Hammerstein were busily writing a new show. But a suggestion put to them by Dorothy Fields for a musical based on the life of Annie Oakley, the girl who frightened more Indians than Calamity Jane, was too interesting to turn down. They were too busy to do the show themselves but they could produce it if someone else wrote the score. Why not Jerome Kern? If he agreed, Dorothy would write the lyrics.

When the script came back—written jointly by Dorothy and her brother Herbert—a copy went straight off to North Whittier Drive. With it was a telegram from Richard Rodgers: 'IT WOULD BE ONE OF THE GREATEST HONOURS IN MY LIFE IF YOU WOULD CONSENT TO WRITE THE MUSIC FOR THIS SHOW.'

Jerry, despite his anxiety, couldn't resist the temptation. In the meantime, he wrote a new number for the *Show Boat* revival—talking about it and humming it over the phone to Oscar in the same conversations in which he discussed his plans for the 'Annie Oakley' musical. The song, 'Nobody Else But Me', suited Oscar perfectly and he furnished a lyric which was ready for Jerry's arrival in New York on November 3, 1945. *Show Boat* was scheduled for an opening at the Ziegfeld Theatre two months later, in January 1946.

Jerry had not told anyone that for the past few months he had been suffering from high blood pressure. Since he disliked bad news himself, he put it to the back of his mind. The idea of the new show was not so easy to bury. Privately, he told friends: 'I'm frightened to death,' but nothing would stop him taking advantage of the big chance he was now being offered. The dynamo inside him was whirring ready for the task ahead. But it *was* a risk; with pictures, he had always had a certain amount of time in which to write his score—and once it was all delivered, he got his very satisfying fee. Any subsequent financial headaches were the studios' concern.

A Broadway show, on the other hand, could take nearly two years to get onto the stage—and then it could die overnight while still in the try-out stage in Boston or Philadelphia. The tension of it all had killed men before, and Jerry's doctor had also warned him against travelling in the cold winter air. But

Rodgers and Hammerstein were very persuasive, and there was no doubt that he wanted the project. He also yearned to get back to New York—and if the new show worked, that was where he was going to live.

He and Eva arrived in Manhattan after the long, comfortable train journey from Los Angeles and checked into the St. Regis Hotel. But Jerry was not relaxed. He had been worried ever since he boarded the train. 'I didn't play "Ol' Man River" before I left home,' he told Eva, who tried to laugh off his superstition, but when she realized how serious he was, started to worry, too. He referred to it constantly over the next couple of days.

His meetings with Rodgers and Hammerstein were very cordial, and although he hadn't yet written anything for the 'Annie' show, he had a good idea of what he would produce for his first 'Western'.

On November 4, he had a quiet early lunch with Guy Bolton at the Hotel Astor. He was not very relaxed, though he ate and drank heartily, and when he had finished, paid the usual compliments to the maître d' and to the chef. But for once he did not ask for any recipes. He and Bolton talked about the possibility of doing a new show together, once 'Annie' was out of the way. 'Well,' Jerry said, 'we've got to be very sure it's going to be a success because otherwise Oscar and Dick Rodgers are going to have the laugh on me.' He was still not altogether reconciled to their recent successes—which, he kept telling himself, might have been his, had he not been so stubborn.

They shook hands and went their separate ways. Eva had gone out to lunch with Dorothy Fields and Jerry didn't want to go back to his hotel just yet. Anyway, he had promised to go to Ackermans and look out for a piece of furniture for Betty. He was ready to haggle with a salesman—it was one of his favourite occupations.

As he crossed from one block to the next, his walk was brisk. He was enjoying being once more on his old stamping ground, thinking about his good fortune, smiling at the policeman and chatting to the newspaper sellers. He reached 57th Street where it joined Park Avenue, and it was at this point, just outside the building of the American Bible Society that he stopped in his tracks. Somehow he couldn't move any further. A second later, he collapsed, and lay unconscious on the sidewalk.

Passers-by saw him fall and called an ambulance. Still unconscious, Jerry was taken to City Hospital. It was on Welfare Island, under the 59th Street Bridge, and within sight of the very house at the corner of Sutton Place and 56th Street where almost 61 years earlier he had been born.

Nobody at the time gave a thought to his identity. He was simply an elderly man who, Dr. Henry Greenberg diagnosed soon after Jerry was wheeled into the white-tiled public charity ward, had had a stroke. The ward was spotlessly clean but the other inmates were some fifty residents of the Bowery and of the doorways of tenements on the Lower East Side. Every ailing derelict from the borough of Manhattan seemed to have been taken there.

A nurse was asked to go through the pockets of Jerry's suit— made of the kind of cloth, she might have noticed, not usually seen at City Hospital. The only piece of identification was a card bearing the letters ASCAP. There was a number on the card, but nothing more. Jerry had not signed it. A hospital secretary rang through to the ASCAP offices where an immediate check was made of the association's records. The hospital official was asked to describe her patient. The realization that both description and number added up to Jerome Kern was greeted with gasps of horror. When the doctor was told, he asked the drunks and derelicts in the ward to behave themselves. They all complied.

The nurse in charge of the ward refused to go home that night. 'Mr. Kern has given me so much pleasure,' she told the senior physician, 'that the least I can do is stay with him.' She remained for 24 hours, keeping a non-stop vigil at his screened-off bed.

ASCAP's secretary had tried to contact the St. Regis, but Eva was still out with Dorothy Fields and no one knew where they were. In the meantime, Jerry was expected at the *Show Boat* rehearsals at the Ziegfeld Theatre, a date he had either forgotten or for which he intended to be late. Oscar Hammerstein's son, Bill, who was auditioning for a part, was asked to ring through to the St. Regis to find out how long he would be.

171

Eva had just returned to her suite. 'I don't know,' she told Bill, 'perhaps he went out for a walk. He said he wanted to do that.' No sooner had she replaced the receiver than the ASCAP official rang through to the theatre with the news about Jerry.

The official followed it with a call to Oscar Hammerstein's Long Island home—but Oscar was actually at the St. Regis, attending a meeting of the Dramatists Guild. With Eva, he immediately rushed over to the hospital where Jerry still lay unconscious. Oscar tried to provoke some sign of recognition from his old friend by singing 'Ol' Man River' to him, but without success.

Friends from all over, people in the music business, fellow art connoisseurs, old school mates, joined the trek to Welfare Island and the same hospital where, almost a century earlier, Stephen Foster had died. Meanwhile, Betty flew in from California, grief stricken. She was greeted with the news that he was holding his own, but that his condition was still critical. He did not give any indication that he knew that she, Eva or anyone else was with him.

Though he was getting the best possible attention from his own personal physician, Dr. Foster Kennedy, Betty asked for her father to be moved to the much more impressive Doctors Hospital on Upper Fifth Avenue. She was afraid of his waking up in an institution and finding himself surrounded by the sort of men with whom he would never have mixed in his life. She called in another doctor, and after two days at Welfare Island, Jerry was moved. In the carpeted private room to which he was taken, he remained desperately ill, although doctors issued public bulletins denying that he had had a stroke and saying that they still had hopes for his recovery.

But at 1 p.m. on Sunday November 11, 1945, with Eva, Betty and Oscar Hammerstein by his side, Jerome David Kern died. He had never regained consciousness.

172

Can't Help Lovin' That Man

THE DAY THAT KERN DIED, President Harry S. Truman spoke of the 'grateful millions' who played his music. His colleague Oscar Hammerstein said in his funeral oration: 'Our real tribute will be paid over many years of remembering, of telling good stories about him and thinking about him when we are by ourselves.' A leading musicologist described Kern's work as being 'like black and white drawings . . . They need no colour, nor ornament to conceal bad drawing or poor craftsmanship. The architecture of a Kern song is always in balance, perfect in form and pleasing in design.'

Olin Downes, a critic on *The New York Times*, said of him: 'Mr. Kern had a technical and artistic background not shared by most of his American colleagues in his field.' A fact willingly accepted by those colleagues, men not easily given to praising a rival.

George Jean Nathan once wrote that Kern was 'quietly and unassumingly writing the most gracious and graceful tunes that have been written in this country since they laid Victor Herbert in the grave.' Quietly? Unassumingly? *The New York Times* described him as a 'modest' man. Surely he was not that. He knew how good he was, and believed in proclaiming the fact. He once told bandleader Paul Weston: 'Young man, if you want to accomplish anything in this business, you must remember that it is extremely important that you meet every suggestion with the word "why", and say it loudly in an aggressive manner. That way, you are a little ahead to start with and in the end you'll get your way.'

Most of his contemporaries are now dead, although Irving Berlin (who took over from him the show that became the hugely successful *Annie Get Your Gun*) is still alive to tell the world how much it owes Jerome Kern, even if the world sometimes forgets its debt. In 1960, seventy-five hitherto unpublished songs by Kern were found in a manilla envelope in a bureau drawer, but nobody rushed to buy them. An attempt to build a show round them failed. Yet eleven years after that find, *Show Boat* had a splendid revival in London, and in 1975 and 1976 *Very Good Eddie* had a stupendously successful revival in both New York and London.

Eva—who married again and lived happily with her new husband—is now dead. Betty lives in Kentucky, a renowned breeder of horses, and the deeply-committed custodian of her father's work. 'They Didn't Believe Me', 'Only Make Believe', 'Smoke Gets In Your Eyes', 'Look For The Silver Lining', 'Long Ago and Far Away', 'All The Things You Are', and 'Ol' Man River' are songs that rank in the world's culture alongside the symphonies of the classicists and the books of the literary giants whom Kern admired so much. His music may have been written long ago and far away, but it still goes rolling on.

Index